G000162157

All too often leadership books and books on edu[...] processes and issues to simple checklists and simpl[...] Myatt, understands that there are many intricate [...] and leading a school. One thing you get from her [...] at the centre of schools. Too often statistics, numbers and policies detract us from the fact that in education we deal with real people, young or old, who are complex and unpredictable. They have dreams. They have fears. They have insecurities too. Humans daily tread the fine line between helplessness and hope. This daily battle is at the heart of the book. How do you turn negativity into positivity?

Mary's book looks at education from the perspective of people. The book isn't about hitting targets and impressing people. The book is about how to make the experience in schools better for students, parents, teachers and leaders. There are schools in the world where teachers feel helpless. There are schools in the world where leaders feel helpless. 'Hopeful Schools' is a welcome beacon of light, hope, and positivity in possibly one of the most challenging times in education. Be clear, this isn't a rose-tinted view of education either. Mary addresses the difficult issues head-on and asks the difficult questions, using a wide range of sources and examples (inside and outside education), which we have to ask ourselves if we are going to be better or the best.

'Hopeful Schools' is a brilliant philosophical investigation into how we can get the best from our students, the best from our teachers, and the best from our schools. It is a book of ideas, questions and examples told with such warmth, detail and thought that only a human could write it. This is about leadership with the heart and the head for doing the right thing.

Chris Curtis, Head of English

'Hopeful Schools' is a breath of fresh air and reminds you 'why' we do 'what' we do, whilst making you think 'how' we go about it.

Mary encourages us to consider what soulful schools; heart-based education and courageous leadership could and should look like.

This book will nourish you and restore your faith in the future of our education system. It will reassure you that by being hopeful we can effect change.

'Hopeful Schools' will inspire you as it will remind you that through resilience, courage and hope we can create school cultures underpinned with trust and integrity.

Hannah Wilson
Headteacher, Aureus School

Another lovely, nurturing and enjoyable easy read from the ever helpful Mary Myatt.

Thank heavens for Mary Myatt who once again takes on the role of caring, demanding big sister; protective and authoritative in her praise of ordinary good teachers against the new establishment bully boys and girls with their negativity and supercilious judgements.

In this book 'Hopeful Schools' Mary Myatt further seals her position as one of the most caring and supportive optimistic and effective voices in English education.

Tim Brighouse, Mick Waters, John West-Burnham relax and enjoy your beckoning retirement for now we how Mary Myatt to support, challenge and inspire teachers to be even better.

Part personal observation, part philosophical, certainly encouraging and with novel references and simple practical examples Mary Myatt serves up another teacher-friendly guide.

Peter Hall Jones
Former headteacher, international education consultant, leadership coach
Founder of the Curriculum Foundation

What Mary Myatt has managed to do here is put the markers down for organisations and individuals in how they define their optimistic and hopeful selves. She dismantles the inhuman machinations of faceless institutionalism and supports its replacement with a genuinely warm, informed and witty alternative. Hope and humanity should be at the centre of what we do. In Hopeful Schools, Mary Myatt shows us how. Essential.

Hywel Roberts
Teacher – Writer - Speaker, Create Learn Inspire Ltd

Dec 2016

*To Catherine
#LearningFirst!
Best wishes
Mary*

First published in 2016

by Mary Myatt Learning Limited
website: www.marymyatt.com

© 2016 Mary Myatt
All rights reserved.

ISBN: 978-0-9956687-0-6

Set and designed by DesignersCartel
www.designerscartel.com

Printed and bound in Great Britain

*For the Ward siblings: Michael, Jane, Annie, Tony and Johnny.
Good souls all.*

Contents

Foreword

Wow! This is an amazing book. I read this from cover to cover in one sitting and I loved it. Mary Myatt's gentle wisdom and humour shines through every page to remind the reader of the positive action and affirmation that emerges when we experience feelings of hope instead of helplessness.

Mary's extensive experience of working alongside teachers and school leaders, enables her to provide reflection on leadership practice that is enabling and supportive of others. She embraces and recognises the vital importance of qualities such as generosity and kindness; convincing us through carefully chosen stories of practice, that when there is hope we not only feel better, we can act to make things better.

This is a 'feel-good' read precisely because it is rooted in reality. We are not swept away on a tide of relentless rudderless optimism. Far from it, we experience through Mary's storytelling, her utter insistence that we only feel better when we fully face our challenges. She never asks us to look away. Instead, we realise that instead of denying difficulty, we need to act. She describes the way that leaders can respond to challenge by supporting their organisation to collaborate with collective purpose borne out of a 'can-do' ethos that includes everybody. Her examples range from the individual child and his need to be noticed, to the extent to which as adults we can act, even when there is temptation to believe that nothing can be done. Instances of horrific global events can make us experience a sense of helplessness, but this book reminds us that when we choose to respond locally through small acts of kindness, we contribute collectively to a wider healing purpose.

Throughout the book, Mary uses real-life, everyday examples of people's actions that embody a series of big ideas. She does not shy away from discussion of painful, challenging events that occur in our lives, but instead focuses on how we can react positively in a manner that helps us to heal. Mary's compelling thesis is that we should never give up. She illustrates this through vividly drawn examples that remind us what happens when we are able to live and work in a culture of optimism, trust and celebration of difference. When we work in schools or businesses where the dominant culture is one of collective endeavour, we can all feel supported to achieve more than any one of us might do alone.

I wholeheartedly recommend this book to you, especially if you are facing particular challenges that may feel almost impossible right now. We are helped to see that we are almost never alone in our anxieties. To read this book is to be reminded that when we face and act on our fears in life, we can begin to diminish them and replace them with lively irrepressible positive experiences that illustrate the power of hope.

Alison Peacock DBE, DL, DLitt
CEO, Chartered College of Teaching

Section One
The case for hope

1 On hope

'Retain faith that you will prevail in the end, regardless of the difficulties, and at the same time confront the most brutal facts of your current reality, whatever they might be.'
James Stockdale [1]

Difficulties face every human being and every organisation. Random events cannot be eliminated. There is complexity and unpredictability inherent in human affairs. Chaos, paradox and dramatic change are on the agenda for everyone and every organisation at some point. The examples in this book do not point to air-headed escapism, but rather to the honest and deep reserves which can be drawn on when facing up to a tough reality.

This book describes situations where hope has been important and where the 'challenge of a difficult task, the pursuit of a clear and compelling goal, personal responsibility for a significant contribution to the overall effort, and individual freedom in the pursuit of one's work provide the primary fuel and source of commitment'[2]. It also promotes conditions where it is the norm to build people up, rather than put them down.

'Hopeful schools: building humane communities' is about the difference that hope makes in overcoming difficulties. It is not promoting a blind optimistic view of the world, but an account of how being hopeful in the face of such difficulties, we release energy and can lift ourselves to a higher standard. And the paradox is that individuals and organisations often achieve more than if the difficulties had not presented themselves in the first place.

---

1. en.wikipedia.org/wiki/James_Stockdale
2. The Soul of A New Machine by Tracy Kidder (1981)

Organisations are, by their very nature, messy and all attempts according to Weick[3] to 'impose complete order and predictability will ultimately fail. Learn, adapt, change, evolve, grow, but don't ever expect to have things under control or to know fully where you're going.'

The difference between honest hope and blind optimism is captured in the Stockdale paradox[4]. Stockdale was held captive as a military officer in the Vietnam war. Frequently tortured during his eight years of captivity, he never lost faith during his ordeal: ' I never doubted not only that I would get out, but also that I would prevail in the end and turn the experience into the defining event of my life, which, in retrospect, I would not trade.' Paradoxically however, while Stockdale had remarkable faith in the unknowable, he noted that it was the most optimistic of his prison mates who failed to make it out of there alive. ' What the optimists failed to do was confront the reality of their situation. They preferred the ostrich approach, sticking their heads in the sand and hoping for the difficulties to go away. That self-delusion might have made it easier on them in the short-term, but when they were eventually forced to face reality, it had become too much and they couldn't handle it.'

Stockdale approached adversity with a very different mindset. He accepted the reality of his situation. He knew he was in hell, but rather than bury his head in the sand, he stepped up and did everything he could to lift the morale and prolong the lives of his fellow prisoners.

In visiting hundreds of settings, I notice that there are some ways of working which seem to provide people with energy and focus, even when things are tough. These settings do not try and diminish difficulties or to gloss over obstacles. Instead they acknowledge them, look at them squarely, figure out how to accommodate them and even grow as a result.

While this is intended for educators, it is helpful to draw on the wider literature describing the conditions in other organisations

---

3. The Social Psychology of Organizing by Karl E. Weick (1969)
4. www.youtube.com/watch?v=FpgLAuZdutM

which create hope rather than helplessness. Google's Project Aristotle[5], for example, attempted to find out what characterised the most effective teams. In two year's of research what they discovered was that the skills of the team mattered less than the relationships between members of the team. They found that the five essentials of effective teams were: psychological safety, dependability, structure and clarity, meaning of work and impact of work. And all of these are underpinned by hope.

In 'Strengths Based Leadership'[6] Tom Rath and Barrie Conchie analysed three million responses to 'StrengthsFinder', developed by Gallup to help people discover their strengths. Based on their findings, Rath and Conchie identified the keys to effective leadership: one of these was meeting the four basic needs of people within an organisation. These four are: trust which encompasses respect, integrity and honesty; compassion which includes caring, friendship, happiness and love; stability which embraces security, strength and support and finally hope where followers look for direction, faith and guidance from their leaders. 'Hope creates an aspirational factor among all the things that you're trying to do in your organisation, and it gives people a reason to commit. Hope suggests that the future will be better than the present, and that what we're doing as an organisation now will contribute toward creating that future.'

To take the three aspects of direction, faith and guidance in turn: people want to know that their leaders know the direction of travel and that it points to a better future. In some of the research from this work, Rath and Conchie found that many leaders were focused on being reactive, rather than proactive. This is not to argue that problems should be addressed swiftly, but if that is all that is happening, then colleagues in such organisations are not supported to see a bigger vision and purpose for their work. So placing the day-to-day stuff in a bigger context, helps colleagues to feel hopeful rather than helpless, because they can see that their daily struggles and achievements are contributing to something bigger.

---

5. rework.withgoogle.com/blog/five-keys-to-a-successful-google-team/

6. www.amazon.co.uk/Strengths-Based-Leadership-Leaders-Landmark/dp/1595620257/ref=tmm_hrd_swatch_0?_encoding=UTF8&qid=1475478681&sr=1-1

People want to know that those leading an organisation have faith in them. As Warren Buffet put it: 'A leader is someone who can get things done through other people' and Rath builds on this: 'If you focus on people's weaknesses, they lose confidence. At a very basic level, it is hard for us to build self-confidence when we are focused on our weaknesses instead of our strengths.' For this to happen, leaders need to talk about how they have faith in people, how they are capable of rising to the occasion and how they have the capacity to surprise themselves.

And people expect guidance. No one knows everything and we can all get better. But guidance is light years away from the critical diminishing of a person or their work. Guidance is framed in terms of 'we can all get better, how do we go about this?' In offering guidance and expecting others to do the same, leaders talk about the times when they had guidance and how this made them better at their work, and crucially, how guidance differs from personal criticism. While the latter is painful, it is also unprofessional: guidance, on the other hand, comes from a place of possibility and provides suggestions for a way forward and shows what might be possible.

This book makes the case that by facing reality squarely, drawing on the wisdom of hope and encouraging the potential in others, it will always prove better to be hopeful, not helpless.

2 The language of hope

'Hope is being able to see that there is light despite all of the darkness.'
Desmond Tutu

There's a subtle difference between taking a Pollyanna view on life, choosing only to see the positive, and talking the language of hope. The difference is this: using the language of hope means doing so in the context of facing reality squarely on the chin. It does not seek to downgrade the seriousness of a situation, it does not look to minimise or dismiss dreadful things nor does it pretend they don't exist. Instead, in the face of these, the language of hope articulates the message, this is how things are, and this is how they might be better.

When this happens, we are able to draw on our deepest strength in order to pull up from the well of our reserves, the capacity and the energy to deal with things and to move forward. It comes from a space of reality and clear-sightedness rather than denial and weakness. Churchill knew how to do this. He wasn't born knowing how to do this - he was shy and had a stammer, both of which he had to overcome in his public life and no more so than at the height of Britain's greatest danger. 'Never before in the history of our country has so much been owed by so many to so few.' 'We shall fight them on the beaches'. What is going on here is that the emergency is held in tension with the capacity to hope. Hope in this case that Britain would not be invaded. But this was not hope based on wishful thinking, but rather on attitude and capacity. What hope is doing here is building the deep resilience which in turn concentrates the mind and which produces coherent action. What would people have been like if those messages of hope had not been articulated? It is likely that the morale and spirit of the country would have been diminished. His mantra of 'never give up, never give up' captured both the severity of the situation and the mindset that the British people are brave and resilient. It secured a strength which might have dissipated into panic and hopelessness. What he managed to do was to hold in balance the severity of the threat and the capacity for determination in spite of that threat.

Critical to the language of hope is acknowledging the difficulty of situations, but neither dwelling on them nor casting blame. When one headteacher of an outstanding infant school was asked to run a junior school which required improvement, her response was 'things can be different'. She set out to ensure that both schools had values which are lived and not just laminated; where there was no blame for prior poor performance but instead an absolute focus on improving provision for all and where the business of moving forward is done daily, not as a one off event.

In this context the work is seen as ongoing. It recognises that there will be setbacks and that some areas of the school still need to improve. For example, while learning behaviour in lessons improved quickly, it took longer for it to improve in corridors and around the school. Importantly, this was not about a completely new broom. While senior leaders and governors were new and some staff left after the school became a trust, there were a significant number who stayed. What appears to have happened with those who stayed was that they could see how things could be different and how their practice could be improved. But because this was done *with* them not *to* them, they could see how they could get better. Some whose practice needed considerable improvement are now leading research networks or coaching others. The point is that they had the capacity in them the whole time, but it needed the structures and the language of hope to shift views of their own practice from 'well, what can I do? and I'm not very good' to one of ' I can do this'.

Carl Jarvis, executive headteacher at Hartsholme Academy and CEO at Eos Education uses the language of hope with his colleagues and with children. And because adults have a healthy dose of hope, they impart this to their children. The Eos philosophy is based on the absolute belief that children are capable of far more than we as adults think they are. An incredibly rigorous curriculum is in place and all pupils are expected to engage with it, some with additional support. Hope here, is linked to expectation. And hope is expressed in the mission statement 'respect, empower, believe, learn, succeed' and importantly it is expressed daily: 'We can do this, it is possible'. The school has emerged from a dull, demotivating curriculum and atmosphere to one of high energy, excitement, enjoyment and concentration. This has come about through talking about how things are possible, how every child has the capacity to achieve and that literally, no child will be left behind. And this is done through talking about hope and living it daily through demanding, no excuses, work, by *all*.

3 Being in the black

'Success has always been easy to measure. It is the distance between one's origins and one's final achievement.'
Michael Korda

There is mostly more going on that is good, than not good. There is a logic to this. Organisations which are not very good either close down, get taken over or go into liquidation. It is the same in education, but we seem to have forgotten this: schools which have let down their communities are mostly closed, taken over or reconstituted. Now, while there are still pockets of schools which are not doing well enough for their children, these are being addressed with much greater urgency.

But it is possible that we have forgotten how far we have come. This has happened at an institutional level and at an individual setting level. Because the world could always be better, we sometimes forget that it already is. It is better in these respects…. and there is still work to do in these….

The imperatives of continual improvement have blinded us to the fact that collectively and individually we have achieved so much. This is an argument for clocking, auditing and monitoring some of the things which we have achieved. This is not about being complacent or self-congratulatory. It is about having a clear-eyed view of where we are and the distance we have travelled. A kind of stocktaking.

So, most children are in school most of the time. Mostly their teachers are pretty good and much of the work they do with their pupils is great. Schools might pause every now and then and produce a collective picture of how things are different from a year ago, from six months ago, a week ago. This helps to clarify just how far they have come. Because in living the work day by day, we do not always appreciate how the small gains build up into large gains. These might be: more children coming to school (a rise in attendance), a greater participation in extra curricular activities (sport, debating, community service), more children doing well in public examinations, strong staff and positive pupil surveys; renewed commitment and energy; revised work practices such as streamlined meetings.

It makes a difference if these are visual. Some settings do this on a time line. Here we were a year ago, and here we are now. What does it look like in comparison? What have we learnt along the way that is good? 'Look how far we have come…' While this is a simple way of monitoring it, it is very powerful because it helps us to understand the agency of the small things, done every day. Too often, the accumulation of the small, growing in to the large, is unnoticed, unacknowledged. And this is a pity, because we can become downhearted by the enormity of what we still have to do. But in slowing down and thinking about how far we have come, we reinvigorate our purpose, our resolve and our energy into taking the next steps forward.

What we are doing when we do this, is we are looking at the bank balance of our work, or an organisation's work. The deposits, in black, are our achievements, our successes. And if we think of them as a bank balance, then they provide the ballast, the security against which to make more investment, in building and creating new things for the future. This is an essential part of being hopeful, not helpless. That the resilience, courage and hope for going forward with our heads held high and with energy restored, is taking full account of and acknowledging the good and great work which has already taken place. The same applies to different aspects of school life. It could be used as a review tool, a self-evaluation tool, an audit. At the moment, these are mostly on a deficit model. This is what we still have to do. But how about listing, clocking and celebrating just how far we have come?

What might be the downside to this? Is it possible to become big headed or complacent? Unlikely. It is possible that the opposite is true - that there is so much to do, how are we ever going to get through it? And, those colleagues and settings which are complacent, smug or big headed, usually get rumbled anyway. So, how does this help with being hopeful, not helpless? In monitoring and celebrating just how an organisation or setting has come, we are reinforcing our resilience and capacity to continue to do more of the same and to do even better. It is a mindset that says, if we can do this, then we can also do that.

The bank balance of being in the black is just a way of looking at our achievements, both at an organisational and an individual level. We could also do the opposite and see what the red, the deficit model, looks like. And this is a healthy thing to do, in order to keep the perspective in balance. However, the main purpose in this context is to secure our resilience, to give ourselves a quiet, or not so quiet, pat on the back. What we notice, we do more of. What we have done in the past, the things that went well, can become the springboard for the next aspect of improvement. It is a security blanket which is there not to make us complacent, but to propel us into spaces and places which are even better.

What sorts of tools are helpful in this exercise? Well, the main thing is that they are not cumbersome or complex. A storyboard might be one way of doing this; this is where we were a few years ago, last year, last month. This is where we are now. The Blob Trees[7] are also a good way of capturing the elements of what it was like at a certain point and what things are like now. They are concrete ways of making concepts and ideas become real. And they give us a real purchase on just how much we have done and how far we have come.

---

7. www.blobtree.com

4 Attention

'To pay attention, this is our endless and proper work.'
Mary Oliver

What we pay attention to usually changes. This is an important aspect of feeling hopeful. If we focus on the misery, our minds become flooded with misery and hopelessness. If we think about all the things that are wrong with our lives, our work and the people we plough alongside, then what follows is that we are attuned to see more of the same. All the things that are wrong as opposed to those which are right. It seems that what we notice produces more of what we notice.

We have all experienced coming across a word which is unfamiliar to us. Then we find we come across the same word shortly after. What seems to be happening is that our brain has made new links and has reset our focus. The things were always there, we just see them in a fresh way, they are brought to our attention. We can only focus on so many things at any one time. What happens when we have an emotional connection with something, is that we set up the neural pathways to short cut other distractions so that certain things come in to our radar. We can use this to our advantage.

What we can take from this is that if we are serious about wanting to focus on hope, we make a point of looking for the good. This is not a rose-tinted, delusional way of looking at the world. It is more a case of keeping it in balance. We are hardwired to notice the bad things that might happen to us. Our ancestors needed to be alert to the physical dangers that might kill them or their young. So hypervigilance is built in to our systems as a survival mechanism. If our ancestors hadn't spotted that lion lurking, they would have been dead meat. So while that level of vigilance was helpful thousands of years ago, it is only helpful up to a point for us today. The sadness in the world is there as a matter of fact. Some of us experience a hefty dose of this. But life is more than that. It is as good as it is bad, as any complex structure is. So, we owe it to ourselves and to our wider experience of the world, to counter-balance the negative by practising noticing the positive.

Linked to noticing the positive, are expectations. Our expectations both for ourselves and for others are a consequence of paying attention as much to the positive as the negative. It is a prosaic observation, but there are two sides to everything. The Janus door, the liminal, the yin and yang, the black and the white. To fully experience life, we need to be open to both. This is why paying attention to keeping an equal balance is important.

So, I can choose to notice that my colleagues were not as co-operative or as open-minded as I'd have liked last time we met. Or I can choose to remember a time when they were fully on board. And perhaps my own attitude conveyed impatience and a rush to crack on. So, by thinking back to a time when things had more flow, when the expectations were high and there was a level of synergy, we are priming our attention to expect more of the same the next time we meet those colleagues. We are priming our attention on the times when we had the conditions we wanted as opposed to the times when they were less productive.

It is the same with children in the classroom. Yesterday, tempers might have been frayed, everyone was under par and things did not go as we would have wanted. Now we can choose to ruminate and worry about that, or we can think back to a few days earlier, when everything was buzzing, all were on task and it seemed as though anything were possible. This is how life is, sometimes the flow is there and everything is good, other times it goes off beam. This is not to say that the rotten days don't matter, they do. But the good days matter too. And if we want more of the good days, it is important that we think about them and let the power of these propel us forward. Like petrol in a car, or a good wind behind us.

If we think about what is likely to happen if we pay attention only to the poor stuff which happened, then when we meet our colleagues or our class the next time, these negative feelings are likely to be expressed in subtle ways: in our body language, in our tone of voice and in our expectations. What we expect is often what we get. For our colleagues and pupils on the receiving end of this, there are very subtle messages which are being conveyed. I am not in a good mood. I expect it will be the same as last time. What's the point? They will pick this up, whether they can articulate it or not. But when we flip it on its head, the opposite becomes the case. We can do this, we can be better. Let's leave the negative stuff behind. Because actually, there is more good than bad in this world. We just have to remember to pay attention to it.

5 Independence

'Every human has four endowments - self awareness, conscience, independent will and creative imagination. These give us the ultimate human freedom... The power to choose, to respond, to change.'
Stephen Covey

There are some complicated aspects to pursuing a line of 'hopeful not helpless.' And two of them are these: hope cannot be forced on others and our own hope cannot be 'done' to others. It is an internal piece of work where we choose to look at the world and our particular situation. In dire situations we might ask ourselves what can be salvaged here, where might this go and why can I learn from it? As a general way of working, we can make a point of finding a purposeful way through rather than deliberately focusing on a deficit model. We choose to look at the expansive possibilities in ourselves, in others and in the wider world.

However, there are many of us and there will be many we are working with, who need additional support. Professor Tom Shakespeare has spoken eloquently about this. As an academic and professor of disability research at Norwich Medical School, he also has achondroplasia, a form of dwarfism. There are many like him who need help with the everyday business of life. And it is likely that for all of us, at some point in our lives, there will come a point when we need to rely on others. This might be as a result of illness, injury or frailty at the end of our lives. It is very unlikely that anyone escapes an episode in their lives when they don't have to rely on others.

For those who need this support every day, there is an interesting dilemma at play. Tom Shakespeare talks about the need for reciprocity. In other words, our need to offer something back in return to the person who helps us. For people who receive help every day, this creates a question of how the help is acknowledged. Often the help is paid for, but there is nevertheless a need to balance the direction of the support with something to offer back. It is likely that when this is denied that the receiver dips into helplessness. In a Radio 4 interview, Tom Shakespeare[8] calls for society to respond to the challenge of delivering help 'without creating domination and infantilisation'.

The thread through this example is that we all crave a degree of independence, a say in our future and a voice in making that happen. This is not about a free for all, carte blanche or a lack of structure. When we translate the idea of reluctant dependency we might consider the expectation that children in school, all children, have a right to make a contribution. This might sound paradoxical, but it is essential, particularly for those children who have additional support either with their behaviour or to enable them to catch up, that they are expected to do something for others. This is not about paying the price for their support, but is rather about sending them the message that they have something unique and important to offer others.

Many schools in fact, are working to these principles - of making sure that they are capturing a full, well-rounded view of their pupils' strengths and areas for development. And as a result of this, ensuring that their strengths are offered to others. So, a child who is an accomplished artist, might be encouraged to do a number of things: design an image to go on a school blog, or website; share with other children how she goes about her work; research the life and work of a famous artist and share it with others. These schools understand that a talent needs an environment for it to flourish and that those pupils with interests should be encouraged to share them with others. And this doesn't have to be a public activity. For shy children who might find it difficult talking to lots of others,

---

8. www.bbc.co.uk/programmes/b07v36ks

that doesn't preclude an expectation that their work reaches a wider audience.

If we accept that reciprocity is something that almost everyone wants to do, then it should help us to see that all children, whatever their level of additional need, have a desire to give back. In hopeful settings, the means and the space are created for this to happen.

Adam Bojelian was born with cerebral palsy and later lost the ability to move and talk. Much of his life was spent in hospital. The only way he could communicate was through blinking. Remarkably, he wrote poems and commentary on the NHS by blinking to indicate the letters of the alphabet to his mother. His poetry achieved global acclaim and his work came to the attention of senior NHS leaders. His parents, carers and hospital teachers created the space for his unique voice to be heard. While all his physical needs had to be met by other people, either professionals or his parents, there was much that he could contribute and his unique wit and voice reached the world. His poetry, stories and sharp observations went out from his hospital bed to the world via Twitter.[9] The actual mechanism for getting his work out was via his parents, in particular his mother, who created a platform for her son and his work. And all she did was to post his words and ideas. While he was confined to hospital, his unique gifts were flowing out to the world. And after his death in 2015 at the age of 15, the archive and legacy of his ideas continue to speak to people across the world. What was happening here is that his parents and professionals saw that he was not just someone who had to be cared for, but someone who also had a contribution to make, about life and living. And without an ounce of self-pity.

In terms of hopeful not helpless, the key message here is that it is one thing to have people believe in me, it is another to have the chance to prove them right and to offer them something on my own terms.

9. www.twitter.com/4AdsthePoet

6 Look at me

'Look at me' is one of the most fundamental desires of the human heart.
Bertrand Russell

Russell's observation might have been driven by his childhood experiences: loss of parents at an early age. Home tutored. Cold grandparents, left to his own devices. Or possibly not. Perhaps he said this because he noticed that people want to be acknowledged. So, if we agree with Russell that one of our basic needs is to be acknowledged, what does this mean for our own needs being met and for considering this in the workplace?

A child playing, trying something new, pushing themselves a bit further than they thought they could. Often the refrain when they are doing this is to call out, usually to an adult 'Look at me, look at me!' In fact this is the need to have a new skill, a new piece of growth acknowledged by someone else. It takes it beyond the child's own uncertain understanding of what they have done; have I really done this? to having the new stage and the achievement acknowledged by another. It could also be that the child's cry of 'look at me' is not just for the achievement, but also for them, as themselves. In that moment they are asking not only for their new achievement to be noticed, but also acknowledgement and affirmation of themselves as a person.

This need to be 'looked at' in an affirming, rather than a negative way carries on into adulthood. Many of the posts on Facebook and Twitter are reflections of our desire to be noticed. Either for the cleverness of our insights, our wit or the fact we are having a fabulous time. And it is good when others acknowledge that. The 'look at me' in this context is healthy. And in the hard-core, real world, it is healthy to want to be noticed as well. However, the 'look at me' doesn't always need to be public. Not everyone is craving the full-blown publicity in a public forum. And no one is craving an insincere response to' look at me'. And the last thing anyone is looking for is a scornful response to 'look at me'.

There are two sides to 'look at me'. The first is recognising our own need for someone, every now and then, to respond to our moments of 'look at me'. When we have done something which has been tough, when we make an additional contribution, when we have made something new, it is good to have another say 'that's impressive'. Like the child, we know in our heart of hearts that this is good 'stuff'. But like the child, we might think it is just in our own head that it's good. So, to have another person say 'look at what you've done' adds a layer of security to our achievement. It also means that we are likely to build on it.

The second side to 'look at me' is to recognise this same need in others. To remember that it felt good when someone looked at us and what we had done and in a sense to regard that acknowledgement as a gift. Then to offer that, when appropriate, to another person.

If we are going to make the case that a dose of responding to 'look at me' is a healthy thing for all of us, we need to think about when this turns sour, when there is a scornful response to the 'look at me'. This is when there is a lack of generosity of spirit, when the need to put another person down, to be spiteful, is more important than building them up. The worst thing one human being can do to another is to hold them in contempt. The 'look at me' is a space where individuals are vulnerable, where they want the unadulterated warmth of another human's estimation of them. And this vulnerability can be exploited so that others can feel 'better' about themselves, by sneering and making unkind comments. This aspect of our psychological makeup, identified by Russell, has the capacity to go two ways.

But assuming it is the opposite, that the 'look at me' is both expressed and responded to honestly, how does this translate into the workplace? First, if we think it is important, we give it out first. We respond to our colleagues' look at me' signals, by noticing, by asking and by affirming their work. The 'look at me' response might be quite low key, just a few brief words between two people. Or it might have a bigger forum, when it is appropriate for someone's work and contribution to have a wider audience. But this needs careful thought. Not everyone craves the limelight. And indeed, the 'look at me' is less about a big splash and more about an honest acknowledgement either of a job well done, a generous act or simply a positive presence.

In the classroom, there are plenty of 'look at me' moments. And they are more likely to be more demanding from the pupils and students who have not had this at home. Every child needs to have one person in their life who will stop what they are doing, to listen to what they are saying. Not at every moment of every day, but enough to know that when they have something important to say, there is a significant person in their life who will take them seriously, who won't sneer or minimise either their triumphs or their sorrows. The teacher in the classroom has a role to play in the 'look at me'. This is the quiet acknowledgement of a child's contribution. Instead of rushing straight on, just the pausing, the nodding, the saying 'that's interesting, can you tell me more', the praise for honest, hard work, done without fuss, are all ways of acknowledging the 'look at me' need in the child. And this doesn't only apply to young children. Every adult, every one of us, needs to know that we are taken seriously. And that there is a space for 'look at me' which is neither vain, nor ambitious, but a simple joy of being recognised by another human being.

Section Two
Attributes of hope

7 Big Heart

'Neither comprehension nor learning can take place in an atmosphere of anxiety.'
Rose Kennedy

How does a big heart help with being hopeful? Well, it is the source of our well-being. It is a way of thinking about the world and about ourselves and the way we conduct ourselves with others.

So what does it mean to have a big heart? In the metaphysical sense it means to be prepared to look kindly on the world and on other people. In fact the universe doesn't much care about us. It is a living thing with the capacity for both devastation and beauty and in order to be fully human, we need to respond to it wholeheartedly. Developing a big heart makes us more alive to the possibilities for growth and for potential.

So how do we go about this? Well, we become conscious of our heart first of all. When we think about those we love, we notice that our heart grows a little, that it expands. Now we are not all meant to be saints, but if we can practise this with those who we are not so close to, there is a subtle shift in our relationship with them. This is not about being soppy or slipping in standards. It is about waking up to the fullness of their potential, which in turn feeds our own.

The generation of goodwill towards others is a big element of becoming hopeful. This is not to blur our vision, or to make excuses for poor behaviour or low standards, but is more a state of being which expects the best to emerge from others. And of course, from ourselves.

What are big-hearted settings like? Well, they are warm for a start. Both physically and psychologically. There is a warm welcome for those arriving at the building. No frostiness, no unctuous subservience, just an honest pleasure at meeting and greeting. Hotels spend a lot of time and investment on getting this right. Most of them. So does MacDonald's, believe it or not. Notice how any member of staff behind the counter greets you and others as customers. They don't muck about. They have been trained to take your order efficiently and courteously. And most of them will look at you. This is a sign that a multibillion-dollar organisation understands the importance of this element of big-heartedness. Now there will always be exceptions to the rule, because that is human life, but by and large I have noticed this to be the case.

And in schools with big hearts, everyone from the front desk to colleagues and children in corridors and classrooms are keen to greet you. Not to hold you up, but to welcome you through the warmth of their demeanour. This happens when they have received big-heartedness themselves. It doesn't create itself, so ultimately it has to be a leadership thing. In fact I would argue that anyone demonstrating big-heartedness is showing leadership. So that could be a child, right?

This costs nothing and is as simple as a way of looking at the world, of seeing it for the magnificence that it is and the beauty and wonder of every human being. It is infectious, once someone has been on the receiving end of it.

And then to the classroom. What does a big-hearted classroom look like? Well it is robust for a start, because difficult, demanding work goes on here. There is no watering down, no soft options, everyone is working hard, struggling but persevering. But every now and then there is a heartfelt laugh, a sense of the ridiculous, a joke or an amusing pun or aside which is responded to by all in the classroom. In big-hearted classrooms, even when the work is very serious, it is possible to have a laugh about it sometimes.

And in big-hearted classrooms, the feedback, critique and analysis is robust and kind, in equal measure. Why would anyone water down feedback just to make someone feel better? When feedback comes from a robust big-hearted space, it can be accepted, used and worked on to improve. Because the intentions come from an honest place. Which help us all to feel hopeful, not helpless.

8 Hard won success

'We shy away from hard work because inherent in hard work is risk. Hard work is hard because you might fail.'
Seth Godin

Success feels sweet. But easy success is hollow. Feeling hopeful comes from knowing that we have done difficult things in the past and managed to do them well. And we surprised ourselves by achieving things we didn't think we could do. So we need to do two things to inoculate ourselves against feeling hopeless when faced with something which feels daunting. We need to trawl though our memories for a few times when we thought something was beyond us and rerun it in our minds. It could be related to our work, to our relationships or to something we do in our own time. Something which seemed really tricky, or uncomfortable, but we went ahead and did it anyway and surprised ourselves with the fact that it went well. This is securing our resilience and setting us up to be hopeful, not helpless for the next big thing.

It could be that we committed to doing a charity walk or run further than we have ever done before, and we just weren't sure how it would go. But we took one step, and then another, and then another. And we did it. Often, with other people for company, doing the same thing. Think back to the feeling of what it was like to arrive at the finishing post. The feeling of exhausted pleasure at a hard job, well done. If we can do something like that in the past, we can translate those feelings of anticipation, tinged with fear before we started, to the pleasure or elation of finishing. And we can apply that to the job we are facing now. That is how we grow, by extending the muscles and doing things which we haven't done before, or going further than before.

And it's painful en route, but the sweet sensation of achievement more than compensates.

For many people, the fear of public speaking is on a par with the stress and sorrow of bereavement and divorce. They would rather do anything than stand up and talk to other people. But those who have felt the fear and done it anyway, also talk about the tremendous rush of adrenaline and pleasure which comes from going through the pain threshold, actually doing it and finding that they survived. So, it is hard won success. But it feels sweet. One of the things to remember about speaking to an audience, is that we talk to people all the time. And most of us are happy to talk to one or two people. Well, a large audience is made up of lots of individuals, so we just need to imagine that we are talking to one or two of them. Another thing to hold in mind is that most people are not out to catch us out. They are interested in what we have to say, and we don't need to be word perfect. In fact, perfection puts people off.

Or we might have done something difficult in our spare time - learnt to ride a motorbike, grown vegetables, cooked a demanding dish, completed a difficult crossword or a challenging puzzle. These are all examples of successes which did not just land in our laps. We had to work at them, put some effort and sweat in and be prepared for them not to work. In other words, being prepared to take a risk. It is in these examples that we learn that success can only be hard won. Things which come too easily are not stretching and strengthening the muscles and sinews of resilience.

How does this translate into the workplace? Well, we shouldn't make things too easy for ourselves, our colleagues or the children we are teaching. Otherwise they won't savour the sweetness of success. It is in the struggle and the uncertainty that the real work goes on. And if things don't work out as we hoped, then we learn from them. It is better to have tried and not got something right than not to have tried at all. Being prepared to fail is one of the conditions for savouring success. Because if everything were certain, we would have no satisfaction when things go well. However, in the workplace and in classrooms, this will only work if we have created the conditions where it is acceptable to make mistakes, to fail and to talk about them. No one wants to be made to feel like a Muppet. And not we ourselves, our colleagues or the children will be prepared to put themselves into a space where they might fail, if they think that they are going to be humiliated. So, we need to work on the conditions for high challenge, low threat, first.

What are these conditions? Well, first they are talked about. This is an important aspect for setting up the space for all of us to succeed. The atmosphere doesn't happen by chance, it is created by the way we do things, talk about success and failure and acknowledge that mistakes are good because they are routes into new learning. We have to make them concrete, by talking about them. People take their cue from others. If other people are prepared to say that it is all right to fail, and exemplify this by talking about their own mistakes, then others will realise that it is acceptable to talk about their mistakes as well. This doesn't happen by chance and it has to come from leaders first.

Then, we talk about the things which we didn't think would go well, when we thought we might fail but which turned out just fine. Here, we are not boasting or blowing our own trumpets, but we are talking about the twin aspects of effort and hard work, which sometimes comes off and sometimes doesn't.

9 Learning without limits

'Our study illustrates how, over the years, we have enabled all children to have the chance to surprise us - and themselves - about what they can achieve'

Dame Alison Peacock

This is an overview of learning without limits, the basic premise of which is that we are all capable of doing more than we think we can; that sometimes we or others put a limit on what we might achieve; that there are ways of setting up learning that meets the child where they are and indicate a way which is more imaginative, more interesting and more powerful than ever thought possible. This, according to Alison Peacock, is possible if we refuse to label children and we refuse to label teachers.

Learning without limits is for everybody. When Alison arrived at Wroxham, hope had been lost. Staff were disheartened, standards had fallen and children were not making the progress they should. To illustrate how learning without limits is for everyone, Alison talks about one child in her TEDx talk[10] . Fostered at a young age after a difficult start in life, his development was behind that of a child expected for his age. After two years at her school, on the advice of educational psychologists, it was agreed that his needs would be better met in a special school setting. Several years later the special school said that they thought he was ready to return to mainstream schooling. With some reservations, due to his complex needs, he returned to Wroxham. Here he flew and achieved level 5 in his SATS (Statutory Assessment Tests). An example of how important it is to be prepared to allow children to surprise us.

---

10. www.youtube.com/watch?v=8oxxPi6c-Nw

What does this have to say about being hopeful? The child's foster parents were hopeful on his behalf, both schools were hopeful too. And this was translated into practice. Not just wishful thinking. And through this, the child became hopeful on his own behalf. Any child, including a child with considerable additional needs, doesn't need saving. They need the highest of expectations without exception. And the support and the resources to get there.

And then there is Vic Goddard, principal at Passmores Academy who speaks with heartfelt conviction about giving every child a chance[11]. A student returned from abroad after difficult circumstances and joined the school in year 9. He had considerable additional needs. In the Channel 4 TV programme 'Educating Essex', this student was filmed at the final graduation, standing up and speaking eloquently about how his time at the school had been the best of his life. His speech was covered in the national media. Miles of column inches were written about him. This student had faith in his future, because people had believed in him.

So, how does this translate into leadership? It is the message that things can and will get better which leaders internalise and then articulate, that make the difference. That while life will often be tough, there are no hiding places for those who are relentlessly hopeful about the future. Starting with today. So wise leaders understand that in order to feel hopeful and to set the scene for their colleagues to learn without limits, they need to find a rock to build it on. The rock that supports the foundations for a future belief of learning without limits. And in essence it is this: if you are already good at something, if you have done certain things well, you can do it again and you can go even further.

So, they make a point of noticing what a colleague has done well. They notice a strength which they have. And they talk about it. Wise leaders draw people out by asking them, can you tell me more about that? How did you do that? Would you be prepared to share that with others? It is this gentle drawing out and helping people to realise that they are better than they think they are,

---

11. www.youtube.com/watch?v=KMfGGX9tY08

which is at the heart of working in this way. And it means that from these foundations it is possible to look to the future. 'Look, if you can already do this, where else might it go?'

Linked to this, they create stories and paint a picture of what the future might look like. How the future can be bigger, and better. And that everyone has a contribution to make to it. What happens when people have their strengths recognised, acknowledged and celebrated they are likely to want to do more. If we have something we are good at, we naturally want to get better at it. The problem is that many of us don't realise that we are really good at an aspect of our practice. Usually because we take it for granted that everyone can do it. And partly because many of us are modest. So we need to be open to taking the honest feedback of those who are giving it. Not out of a sense of false pride, but as an honest acknowledgement of our gifts, hard work and practice.

And in the classroom, there are big implications for learning without limits. This philosophy encourages children not to be labelled. Their needs and barriers to learning should be identified but this is different from labelling them. A staggering statistic from Gordon Stobart in 'The Expert Learner'[12] showed that 88% of 4 year olds placed in sets were still there by the end of their schooling. What would have happened if Alison Peacock had used sets? Where would the child with additional needs be? It's very unlikely that he would have reached the top scores in his SATS.

We do not truly know what anyone is capable of until they are given interesting and difficult things to do. So a 'learning without limits' setting ensures there are interesting, thought-provoking, challenging things for children to do. And that alongside this there is plenty of appropriate support and timely feedback. If children are engaged in thoughtful, absorbing practice, they are both paying attention to the now, are in the moment and are also on the path for a bigger story, which moves them into tomorrow and the future. Feeling hopeful is a by-product of interesting, deep work. It manages the delicate double act of engagement in

---

12. www.amazon.co.uk/Expert-Learner-Gordon-Stobart/dp/033524730X

the present and a deep commitment to the future. 'I'm hopeful because I'm engaged in interesting things and I'm looking forward to doing more tomorrow'.

10 On testing

'Science is curiosity, testing and experimenting.'
Venkatraman Ramakrishnan

How on earth can testing help us feel hopeful? Well, when we put ourselves under a bit of pressure, to do something we find difficult, to go through where we might have got something wrong, we are able to clock very clearly how far we have come. Just one additional correct response helps us to realise that with a bit of application, stuff can stick and that we can get better.

This is how it works. We might read something which we need to be learning about. We then make notes of the key points. We then ask ourselves to describe the key points without going back to the original piece. How much did we remember, how much was missing? In the process of trying to recall we are doing two things. We are setting up the conditions for the neural networks to be stronger, to make sense of the material, so that it remains in the long-term memory and we are able to recall it at a future date. The very process of testing ourselves, under the right conditions makes us brighter. But the second thing it does is that we are able to see very clearly just how far we have come. This is what I was able to recall at the beginning. Having checked, reread and tested myself again, I can see the difference. This builds resilience at the deepest level and provides the bedrock of hope that, with a bit of effort I can get better, I can see how I might improve this in the future. Daniel Willingham[13] has written about how testing can improve performance, and interestingly, one of the findings from the small-scale research was that frequent testing resulted in less rather than more anxiety.

Tests are an unavoidable fact of life. Whether it is for a driving test, school examinations or professional qualifications they are

---

13. www.danielwillingham.com/daniel-willingham-science-and-education-blog/testing-helps-maintain-attention-reduce-stress-in-online-learning

an indicator of proficiency. A marker that something has been achieved. And they are usually dreaded because the stakes are high, either we pass or we don't. But the kind of testing referred to here is the self-testing where no one is watching, no one is criticising and no one is making us feel inadequate. We are creating our own conditions for checking what we know, understand and can do. It is a private matter and no one is going to check whether we have passed or failed. This is the important distinction. Testing is being used as a deliberate tool to help us improve. And in doing so, help us to feel hopeful, not helpless. If I couldn't grasp this before and now I can what happened? I put a bit of effort in and I improved. It is as simple as that.

How might this work in the classroom? Well the first thing is that the high stakes element has to be removed. There should be no penalties for getting something wrong. This is just checking what we know and what we need to do to improve. Tests can provide a very concrete way for children and their teachers to see their progress. Particularly when the results are monitored over time. They are the fundamentals of ensuring that children have the basics. We couldn't do our six times tables two weeks ago, but now we can. The language around this is really important. In describing this work to children, it is important that this is not about failure. It is about checking what we know, what we don't know and to see how far we have come on the one hand, and how far we can go on the other.

The element of improvement and competitiveness needs to be set against what the child could or could not do before, and what they can do now. This is not about measuring children against one another. These are personal, not public, milestones. But they help to make the learning visible.

The bottom line is, 'I couldn't do this before, and now I can.' Making the progress visible is a fundamental aspect of supporting children to feel hopeful not helpless. It also helps to support meta-cognition and talking about the learning. What was it that made the difference between then and now? What did I do to get this level of progress? What was the effort I put in? What were the things I used to help me to get better? What does it feel like to see how far I have come? And in doing this, we support children to be hopeful, not helpless.

One of the ways to minimise the potential threat and fear of this, is to get children to set their own tests. What do they need to get sharper at? What do they need to improve? So, there might be a generic test for the whole class. And as a result of that, what do individual children need to practise to get right next time? This means that the teacher is holding the bigger picture, whether it is times tables or spellings and then allowing children to self regulate by realising that there are some things which they need to go back and do again. This turns it into a journey of improvement rather than a shallow test. And it is deeply satisfying, because the evidence is there for the child as an individual to see and to take pride in their improvement. There is no shame in not knowing something; there is only shame in not trying. It is in the trying that deep learning takes place, in the retrieval of information that secures long-term memory. And once the initial lack of confidence is overcome, it becomes deeply satisfying and as a by-product of that actually enjoyable. It moves from feeling hopeless to hopeful and is a way of working which will have implications beyond the classroom. We need to encourage our pupils to say 'I just need to go back and revisit this'. Because it is in the revisiting that the learning goes deeper.

11 Facing tragedy

'It's not what happens to you, but how you react to it that matters.'

Epictetus

Being hopeful, not helpless is not about closing down our awareness of terrible things happening. Instead, it faces them squarely to find a way of reconciling them, making sense of them and integrating the pain. There are two examples which come to mind. The first is the bombing of a hospital run by Médecins Sans Frontières in Syria. The bombing resulted in deaths and injuries of civilians, patients and medical staff. While an enquiry found human and systems errors were to blame, there are still questions about whether an international enquiry is needed and whether the bombing constituted a crime against humanity. The enormity of the tragedy and the news of it can leave us feeling hopeless, so far away and unable to make a difference. So, when news like this and other similar tragedies happen, the question is, what is an appropriate response and how can we hold on to being hopeful, not helpless. Doesn't this all seem a bit trite, under the circumstances?

I believe there are two main things we can do. First, we can hold in our thoughts those who have been affected. We cannot physically go there, this is neither practical nor desirable. What could we actually do, unless we are medics or specialists in catastrophes? But virtual empathy, the holding of sadness for a short while is a way of sending support. I don't believe it is wasted. It links to our deepest need for connection with others. However, thoughts and good wishes need to be translated into action. Otherwise they remain empty gestures. They need to be grounded in the physical act of doing something. This might be through supporting a charity or contributing to an emergency fund which provides practical help to those affected. And there is also another way to make such sympathy concrete. It is by doing something for someone closer to home. The noticing of someone who is sad, or who we know is lonely and making an effort to say a kind word. To listen to them, to do something for them, is a way of grounding the need to do something on the other side of the world. So how does this help exactly, with the suffering of those on the other side of the world? Well, it doesn't directly. But if we think of global suffering as something which can be mediated and ameliorated through small gestures, so that the sum of suffering is smaller, then our small acts do make a difference to the global suffering pot, even if not directly to the people we were originally holding in our thoughts. We are shifting the focus to where we can make a difference. The suffering in the world will be slightly less through an action, a gesture or a comment on our part. And for us as individuals, it does two things. It ensures that we do not shy away from the horrors, but we look at them squarely, and it also gives us a route to do something, which in the grand scheme of things does make a difference. And as a result, it is possible to feel hopeful not helpless.

The second example of facing tragedy squarely, is that of a headteacher with a student who had committed suicide. Deaths of students are more common than they should be and the tragedy of a life cut short is particularly sharp. Holding hope in these situations is very difficult. Particularly when it is so close to home, when the young person leaves a gaping hole, not just in their family, but in the wider community and the school in particular. Talking to this headteacher, it was possible to see how he was holding the tension between being hopeful, not helpless. This is what appeared to be going on: the school community was in deep mourning and sorrow both for their own loss and in sympathy for the deep distress of the family. He described how this had been allowed to be expressed, through tears, talks in tutorials, remembering the individual at the start of lessons. An honest and appropriate acknowledgement of distress, felt as much by adults as by children. This is a difficult balancing act, because while the grief and pain need to be expressed, they can sometimes turn into self-pitying hysteria. This happens when the expression of pain becomes a thing in itself and breaks anchor from the original source of sorrow. This is not healthy. As a wise leader, he understood this balance and was ready to reassure his community that sadness and its expression have its place. But that hysteria does not.

So the holding of the helplessness was vital in locating a space from which to be hopeful. In asking the school community how they wanted to acknowledge their loss and celebrate the life of their friend, what would they like to do? What practical concrete things could be done that would both hold the sadness and find a path to future hopefulness? Not in some trite superficial way, but in holding the contradictions in balance. He described with warmth how the school formed a guard of honour at the funeral, how tributes of poems and writings were created and collected for the family. How the planting of a tree in the school grounds, chosen by students, including the family in the ceremony, made concrete the mixed emotions of grief and hope. Through his subtle, humane and intelligent reading of what was happening, including his own grief, he walked the path from helplessness to hopefulness.

12 Scarcity versus abundance

*'Not what we have but what we enjoy, constitutes
our abundance.'*
Epicurus

We are hard-wired to notice scarcity. For most of our time on earth, resources to survive have been in short supply. And for some people, in some parts of the world, they still are. Scarcity and danger were constant companions for much of our history. But, for most of us living today, that is not the case.

When we focus on what is missing we are less capable of noticing the potential for what might be. Getting into the habit of looking for what is good is one way of helping us to feel hopeful, not helpless. In organisations which have the scarcity mindset, relationships are often characterised by competitiveness rather than co-operation, where there can only be one winner and the rest are losers. In these settings, it is sometimes the case that coming first becomes more important than doing the right thing. Competitiveness itself is not a bad thing, as it is one of the drivers for improvement, in providing better products and services, in becoming generally better. But when it is one colleague out to beat another, it is less healthy because the mindset is: there is only so much acclaim or prestige and I must get it whatever the cost.

What happens when an organisation shifts from a scarcity frame to an abundance frame? For a start, mistakes are not seen as the end of the world. Most of the mistakes which are made both by organisations and by individuals are not life-threatening. Mostly, they can be rectified as long as two things happen: one, it is acceptable to own up to mistakes without the fear of ridicule or humiliation and two, everyone asks themselves what can be learnt from this. The abundance mindset allows us to imagine what it might be like next time, and to act on that, rather than focusing on all the things that have gone wrong. Learning from mistakes and doing something about them, is a fundamental for feeling hopeful, not helpless.

The organisations which have embraced this actually encourage mistake-making. Not because creating chaos is a good thing in itself, but because through getting to good work, things often go wrong. Organisations and individuals who own up to mistakes often build up long-term trust, because the default mechanism for many is to cover up, to deny and to refuse to respond. Those that do, convey a refreshing honesty, which is a way of signalling that we are serious about what we do, that we want to get things right in the future. Customer service theory has it that a dissatisfied customer is the best way of creating trust in a brand. As long as that customer's concerns and complaints are dealt with fairly, it results in the underpinning of good, honourable, commercial relationships.

Similarly, in individuals, those who have an abundance mentality do not hoard their ideas or suggestions. They are prepared to share them, even if it makes them feel vulnerable, because they understand that there are always more ideas and suggestions, and that one idea that doesn't go down well, is not the end of the world. Again, those who have great expertise and experience in one area are prepared to share that with others, when they are coming from a space of abundance. Their contribution is always: how can we make this better, how can I help others, what have I got to give? The irony is that in giving themselves and their ideas away, they are accruing more from others. Not that they do it for this reason. They do it because they know that abundance is a more productive and healthy place to be, rather than one of scarcity. Individuals who think and work in this way, tend to feel more hopeful than helpless about their own futures.

In the classroom, teachers who work to abundance rather than scarcity principles know that however badly things have gone one day, it does not mean that their practice will always be like that. They know that on reflecting on their work, they can tweak it to make it better. They understand that the focus on abundance and more good things to come is a way of getting stronger. They also know that anyone who has done anything worthwhile has gone through moments of despair and despondency, but that these are not lasting when the wider ocean of abundance comes in to play.

And they model this for their pupils. They reassure them that if anything goes wrong in the classroom, that it is not the end of the world; that there is always the next lesson to get things better. And to enjoy the process in the meantime. They encourage their pupils to see all the good things in their lives, including having them as their teacher, to honour nature, to savour the moment and to look forward to the future. They emphasise the fact that there is enough for everyone. That friendships are not limited to just one person; that human love is not reduced by being shared and that there is more good than bad in the world.

Leaders who understand abundance, notice it and talk about it. They don't keep quiet about the things which are going well. The potential is there for all to improve, to find more satisfaction in a job well done, to make a contribution.

13 Confidence in the future

'Learn from yesterday, live for today, hope for tomorrow. The important thing is not to stop questioning.'
Albert Einstein

This is about looking squarely at life. It is tough and magical in equal measure. We are hard-wired to notice the sad, bad things, because in our earliest history we would be dead if we didn't. Einstein's quote captures this. We have stuff to learn from yesterday, both positive and negative. But we only have this moment, now, to live in. And it's a pity if we don't expect and hope for a better world tomorrow. As creatures with brains, the key to getting the balance is to keep questioning.

So, what were the things that went badly in the past? What can we learn from them? And, just as important, what can we learn from the things that went well? What can we take as nuggets from yesterday that will make today better, more rounded, more productive and more rewarding? And how can we hold on to those so that we are hopeful for tomorrow?

This is a tough call. Particularly when there has been a life-changing event, a bout of depression, a physical illness or loss of a job - when things really do appear to be going from bad to worse. But the fact is we are still here, still alive. And so we owe it to ourselves and those around us to attempt to have confidence in the future. So how does that translate into practice? Well, it starts with a brief stock take of the assets in our lives. Assets in the widest sense: physical, mental, social, emotional, spiritual.

Most of us have somewhere to live. Most of us have the ability to think, to speculate, to read and to write. Most of us have some friends and family. These are all assets and we might consider them as being in the black as far as our 'life' bank balance is concerned. The question is: how do we set these against the insecurities which we all face? The prospect of redundancy, illness, falling out with family and friends. Well, we have a choice. We can either focus on a deficit model of all the things that are lacking, or we can spend a bit of time reflecting on and drawing strength from the things which we do have.

The shift in focus on the things we already have provides some insulation and protection against the things which are missing or which are going badly. There were never any guarantees that life would be easy, or comfortable or secure. But the fact that we are alive should be the basis for hope. How though, do we stop this being some Pollyanna wish list? We do this by keeping to the discipline of holding the positive and negative in balance, and as a result, over time, we are more likely to have confidence in the future.

Many leaders understand the importance of holding this tension in balance. They have a strong sense of history, of where their setting, whether a business or a school has come from. And when it has come from failure, or near failure, they make a purposeful decision to acknowledge the past, but to set the direction firmly in the future. They see the past history and the future story of their organisation as chapters. The past is over. The future is all there is.

Sir Iain Hall is clear about this. As an education strategist and former headteacher, he sees the potential in failing settings. And transforms them. Having set up the King's Leadership Academy in Warrington, his Great Schools Trust took on the running of a school in Liverpool. It had been in special measures for several years and was due to be closed. It serves one of the most disadvantaged areas of the country. It had been a dangerous place to work for students and adults. The behaviour was out of control. Standards for students were at rock bottom. Some essential parts of the curriculum were not being taught. It was on a downward spiral to extinction.

Sir Iain models hope. Pragmatic hope. He and the new principal brought in new leaders, set up structures for governance, leadership accountability, behaviour and standards in teaching. They underpinned this with a dose of high expectations, hope and hard work. These are captured by the trust's ASPIRE code: Aspiration and achievement, Self-awareness, Professionalism, Integrity, Respect and Endeavour. The trust expects all staff to model these in their work. Furthermore the school requires all pupils to sign - in front of their parents - this code of conduct and promise to uphold its values. The systems were put in place quickly, expectations for all working there were raised and the joyful, hard work began. Underpinning it all was a mantra of the future being more positive than the past.

And the result of this extraordinary, purposeful, efficient focus on the future? Within six months of taking over the academy it had moved from being inadequate and in danger of closing, to a school where many aspects of its work were recognised as good and with outstanding capacity for further improvement. There was no magic bullet. Only a laser-like focus on diagnosing what had gone wrong, what was missing and shifting the perspective of everyone to the future. And critical to this acknowledgement of past failure, was that there was no blame. The past is the past and it is only today and tomorrow which count.

What did students and adults now working at this school have to say? Students said that they now enjoyed coming to school, that the high expectations of their teachers were making them engage more and try harder with their work. They all said that behaviour was better and that they enjoyed their learning. What they produced both in terms of what they said in lessons and in their written work was thoughtful, careful, extended and of an exceptionally high quality. Some students who arrived at the school with low attainment were on track to achieve the highest grades.

And the adults working at the academy echoed this. Many were new, but many too had been there when it was in danger of closing. They were working hard, but it was paying off. Everyone was pulling together. There were no passengers. Why? Because one great leader had given them a new story, one they could relate to at the deepest level. That of hope and confidence in the future.

14 No need to be right all the time

'I'm sorry, if you were right, I'd agree with you'.
Robin Williams

Something interesting happens when we place a very high premium on being right, every time. It means that when we are not right, we can slip into the mindset of helplessness. While it is sweet to be proved right, when it is a high stakes mentality it means that when we aren't right, we feel downhearted. Nothing wrong in feeling downhearted *per se*, that is part of life. But the being right can become part of our emotional measure of happiness. And if this is the case, it cannot last. Because there will always be times when we are not right. It becomes a situation of black and white, of feeling good, or not.

This way of looking at things is often when we are precise about the details. Maybe some protocol or accurate fact which was later found to confirm that we were correct. This is a sweet pleasure and no harm in enjoying it. But when it goes the next stage and we feel vindicated, it can easily turn into contempt for the person with whom we are contesting it. We are coming from a space of scarcity and lack of generosity. And the consequence of this is that when the tide turns against us, we are less likely to bounce back because we have placed too high a premium on being right, rather than being generous.

Leaders in healthy organisations understand this. They know that the 'being right' mentality can get in the way of imaginative thinking and can lock colleagues in to a space of feeling helpless, rather than hopeful. Because the stakes of needing to be right, all the time, can result in a reluctance to take on new ways of thinking and working, because the security of 'rightness' can be diminished in these, more expansive circumstances.

So, there is a paradox at work here. The loss of security in the short term about being right, can lead to a healthier attitude over time, which means more rightness can emerge in the long term. The being right is no longer tied up with personal identity, but more with doing the right thing, over time and getting the processes and products right, over time. This is the critical thing. Over time. It is not about winning every battle, scoring small points and petty victories. These belong to the territory of helplessness. It goes like this: I need to claim every victory which comes my way, make a big song and dance about it, in order to make myself feel better. But the problem is that this only serves to make our lives more fragile. Because the sweetness of being right is often short-lived and is likely to be threatened when the next rightness stakes come along.

It also means that we invest a lot of thinking and energy into being right, rather than doing the right thing. It is tempting and it's natural, but it is short lived. Not only does our own state of helplessness increase, we are likely to irritate others as well. They are less likely to confide in us, share uncertain ideas or new ways of working because they are concerned that it might turn into a contest between being right or wrong. Wise leaders cut through this, by example. They talk about the times that they have got things wrong, when the other side won the argument and that they have lived to tell the tale. By taking this route, even though it might appear on face value to be putting themselves down, they are actually showing self-esteem and self-worth and the very fact of not needing to be right all the time.

When others see this, they relax into a more expansive space which means that possibilities are more likely to emerge, more creative ways of solving a problem and the state of play shifts from feeling helpless to hopeful. Because no one needs to be right on every count, every time.

This way of thinking translates into classrooms as well. If children believe they need to be right every time, it diminishes their capacity to learn from their mistakes. And indeed to learn in depth at all. Some of this attitude might have come from the home. And that is not to denigrate children's backgrounds. Many of them come from homes which are very competitive both in sport and in other areas. This is healthy, up to a point. But when the worth and happiness of a child is tied up with being right and winning every time, not only do they shift into the territory of feeling hopeless and helpless, rather than hopeful, over time it reduces their capacity to work on areas for improvement and to improve. The paradox of needing to be right means that the capacity for improvement diminishes.

So clever teachers are clear in their classrooms about the different types of being right. It is good to get the right answer. But if we get the right answer every time, what have we really learned? Because the work was probably too easy. So they strike the balance between enjoying the moment of being right on something and putting it in its context. They also talk to children about how most learning takes place when we have to think hard. And this is different from being right. That thinking hard, often means learning something and forgetting it. Which means in the short term we are not right, we are wrong. But the conundrum in all this is that if we move from the hopelessness of needing to be right all the time, to a space where we are prepared to persevere, we are learning properly *and* in the long term. In talking about this, the wise teacher is helping their children to move to feeling hopeful, rather than helpless.

15 You never know the good you do

'I believe that every human mind feels pleasure in doing good to another.'
Thomas Jefferson

There's an assumption that we need to have hard evidence that something has 'worked' and that we have had an impact. We usually expect this to be in fairly short order. But it might be helpful to think about impact over the longer term. When we think back to those who have had an impact on us, it is not just those who we interacted with today, but also those in the past who have given us encouragement and hope.

This is not about a fanfare. There was an interesting post from English leader Chris Curtis[14] about how he does not make a song and dance at the GCSE results day. There are no public displays of affection. Why not? Well, because this is not his style and he is mindful of those students whose results were not as brilliant as some of their peers. The crowing and loud jubilation can be hard to swallow for those who did not get the results they wanted or needed. Instead, he remains inscrutably the same, whatever the outcomes for the students in his subject. There are a number of reasons for this: first, it is because they are the students' results, not his or his colleagues'; and second, because he knows what it is like when things have not gone so well. So he takes both great results and less than stellar results in his stride. However, the interesting thing is he acknowledged in his post that his students know what he really thinks; that he has their best interests at heart and that he encourages them quietly. Having met Chris, he has an understated

---

14. learningfrommymistakesenglish.blogspot.co.uk/2016/08/public-displays-of-affection-floating.html

warmth and integrity which draws people to him. He has a quiet aura of someone who knows what they are about, who listens carefully and who gives thoughtful responses. He writes brilliantly about what he does in his classroom. My guess is that he has huge impact on his students and their love of his subject just by the way he goes about his business. It is likely that hundreds of students who come into contact with him, will have been and will continue to be influenced by him. It is also likely that he will never really know the extent of the good he is doing, and the good he has done. And he probably doesn't much care. Which is kind of the point.

The gist of this is that it is the way we go about our business, the tenor of our conversations, the kindness and firmness with which we speak to others, does have an impact. We just won't get the feedback. The feedback thing is a double-edged sword. If we are constantly looking for it, we can become needy. Equally, if we pay no attention to it, we are less likely to learn lessons from it. And by lessons, I mean good lessons. If we understand that people are watching us and how we conduct ourselves, we are more likely to make sure that our conversations and our dealings with people are always courteous. That we quietly acknowledge the contribution that others are making and reflecting back to them the difference they make to us. It is as simple as saying, 'I really admire you for that…'. And importantly when someone says the equivalent to us, we shouldn't brush it off through modesty. It is an opportunity to reflect on why that might be so. Without hubris or pride, but because if we are adding value to relationships, to the success of the setting, then we are mindful to do more of it.

The converse is also true. The throwaway remark, the dismissive comment can cut the soul. It might not be meant that way, but the person on the receiving end might be discouraged, diminished and less likely to make a contribution in future. And this is why we should be so careful about what comes out of our mouths and indeed from our emails and messages, when a carelessly written message can have a devastating effect. It is possible to agree to disagree respectfully, to note the other's position. And things might even get heated, which is fine. Because we care about things. But the underlying respect for another's point of view is the critical thing here. When there are tough discussions going on, the way they are conducted is likely to leave a legacy. Where there is a sour note of scorn or contempt for the other's point of view, this is likely to linger on. However, the same conversation might be undertaken in a spirit of respect and where appropriate, a lightness of touch and some humour.

The end of year cards and presents to teachers often reflect this idea of 'not knowing the good you do'. Teachers are often surprised by the warmth and the details which students and pupils give them: the difference they have made to understanding difficult ideas, the way they helped them to get better at their subject, the increase in confidence which they now have. And the warmth with which they conducted their lessons. The important thing is to take note of these carefully, to deposit them in the bank of 'good things' about our practice, rather than take them as superficial compliments. If we think hard about what these young people are saying, we are likely to ensure that our practice in future builds on these strengths.

The bottom line here is that we all have much more influence than we think we have. This is nothing to do with rank or seniority. It is all to do with the way we are. No bells, no whistles, just an honest engagement with work and with the people, young and old that we interact with. The good we do can go on, and on…

16 Outside and inside

'You may not control all the events that happen to you, but you can decide not to be reduced by them.'
Maya Angelou

It can be very easy to be overwhelmed by the state of the nation. High levels of deprivation, domestic abuse, neglect, lack of support for many children at home. And yet there is another way of considering this. To be very clear in our own minds that there are limits to what we can and can't do. We cannot do anything about wider society, nor anything about government policies (until it comes time to vote) nor wider factors which might seem to be counterproductive to a healthy and happy society. But if we acknowledge this and take a robust line about it, we then need to turn our focus on the things we can do. Which do make a difference to children's outcomes.

Let's take three of these and see how they shape up when we focus on the difference we can make. First, the fact that most (but not all) children from poorer backgrounds start school with lower levels of literacy, auracy and oracy. There is much research which show that they are likely to have heard up to 30 million words fewer than children from better off backgrounds. This is a shame, because it is through playing with words, making meaning and experimenting with ideas and thoughts that we learn. However, instead of bemoaning this and saying 'what can we do?' we need to think of all the things we can do during the time our children are with us. So, we need to ensure that we are providing a curriculum which is language-rich. Which is underpinned by the joy and playfulness of words. Which provides an entitlement for every child to hear stories, poems and songs every day. Which does not dumb down, but uses technical words and expects children to use them themselves. In full sentences. A curriculum which encourages children to speculate, to play with words, to take joy in saying and singing them aloud. And a curriculum where teachers and assistants both speak clearly, listen carefully and expect their children to do the same.

A second area is in maths. Many professionals are prepared to admit that either they do not like, or consider themselves 'no good' at maths. In this they are echoing wider society's lack of confidence in maths. And they do this in a way that they would be ashamed to admit that they cannot read or write. This needs to be nailed, very firmly. Numeracy is as important as literacy and yet it is often the poor cousin. Usually for the reasons above. While it does not underpin every aspect of the curriculum in the same way that literacy does, it is nevertheless an essential area to be mastered, not only for its importance in every day life but also for its intrinsic interest and beauty. We need to get ourselves into a state of 'hopefulness' rather than 'helplessness' when working to get numeracy to the same level of status as literacy. One thing which worries people is that it always needs to be precise. Well, in arithmetic precision does matter. But wider maths is concerned with the relationship between things, with pattern, order and sometimes chaos. One way to overcome the concern with 'getting it wrong' in maths is to play with numbers in the way that we are prepared to play with words. Fermi questions are a good way of starting this. Fermi was a physicist and mathematician who wanted to encourage people to think more imaginatively about maths, without being constrained by fear of 'getting it wrong'. His Fermi questions cut across this, by encouraging people to speculate about what a number might be, rather than expecting a precise answer. There are hundreds of Fermi questions but his classic is: 'How many piano tuners are there in New York?' Here, we have to guess a number of possible factors: the approximate number of people living in New York, roughly what percentage of these might have a piano, how often a piano might need tuning and how long it would take a piano tuner to tune a piano. By making rough estimations of these, it is possible to come up with an approximate number. The point is not to be precise, but to play around with some of the variables. In some schools, children are asked: 'If everyone in this school ate an apple every day, how many pips would there be by the end of the week?'. In this example, the children have to ask who is 'everyone'? The adults, the caretaker, the school cat? Is anyone allergic to apples? What is a week - every school day or including the weekend? What is the average number of pips in an apple? In doing this, children are learning to speculate without needing a precise answer. And in doing so come to see some of the fun of playing with number.

The third example comes from Chris Watkins' work at the Institute of Education in London. He and colleagues did research into the levels of violent crime, as captured by police sources in the local area to certain schools. They then compared these with the levels of poor behaviour, including exclusions for those schools. What they found was that those schools with very high levels of crime outside the school gates, did not necessarily correlate with high levels of poor behaviour and disengagement within the school. The difference they discovered was in the way that wider crime and problems in school were referred to and discussed by staff. Where problems in school were 'owned' by the staff, in other words saying 'there is a problem, how are we going to solve it together', there were lower incidents of poor behaviour. In these schools, teachers and leaders were not tempted to say 'Well what can you expect?' or 'It's the fault of their families or the local community'. Instead, they knew the limits of what they can do in wider society and instead took ownership of the problems as they arose in house. Without blame, without finger-pointing and without looking for excuses elsewhere. Showing that it is possible to be hopeful rather than helpless, in tough circumstances.

17 The ethic of everybody

'Inclusive, good-quality education is a foundation for dynamic and equitable societies.'
Desmond Tutu

Dame Alison Peacock used this phrase when she was speaking at ResearchEd in September 2016. In talking about the work she had done over the years with Cambridge University and others, they identified that one of the strands of her work was an 'ethic of everybody'. What might be meant by this and how might it relate to being hopeful, not helpless?

If one of our deepest needs is to belong, then how does this relate to the ethic of everybody? It is the *quid pro quo* or the counterbalance of recognising our own need to belong and extending that to others. What we recognise we need for ourselves, should in turn be offered to others. The settings where this is understood are hopeful.

How does this translate into practice? It means that everyone has a voice, that everyone's views are explicitly sought, that everyone counts. Does this result in a free for all? Is no one in charge? No, the position statement of 'everyone has a voice' does not mean that anything and everything goes. It is instead, an attitude adopted by leaders and adults that things will be done with the best interests of everyone at heart, not that everyone will get their way.

To unpack 'ethic' a bit further. Ethic refers to the way we do things here, the manner in which we go about our business. It also has a layer of moral overtone to it - what is the right thing to do, what is the fair thing to do? And It is the combination of these two which contribute to the idea of 'the ethic of everybody' - doing the right thing, for the right reasons, for everyone.

Easy to say, harder to do. At a strategic level, school leaders including governors might ask themselves whether their work is underpinned by doing right by everybody. This might sound a statement of the obvious, but it comes into sharp focus when leaders are considering the distribution of funds - do the SEN groups get adequate funding - in most schools they probably do, but are the voices of children on the SEN register heard at a strategic level? Have leaders taken the trouble to ask those pupils what they think about their provision and what could improve it? Have they done similar exercises with other groups of children - the high prior attainers, the children with English as an additional language, the children who have a disabled parent or sibling at home? What is it like being at the school for them? If leaders are going to subscribe to an ethic of excellence, they need to have some checks to see whether their aspiration is tracked through and experienced at ground level.

If we think it is worthwhile looking to be hopeful rather than helpless, then subscribing to the 'ethic of everybody' and checking that colleagues and children, indeed everyone, including the cleaning staff, caretaker, lunchtime supervisors and the school cat, does feel included, lifts the atmosphere, creates energy and possibility.

At the classroom level, what might the ethic of everybody look like? For one thing, the meaning of the words are unpacked. What does 'ethic' mean? What does the Greek mean, what might that mean in this classroom? Why is this important? Do we think it is important to include everyone? If we think it is important, what are we going to do to ensure that it happens? Some schools which are working on this, talk about what it feels like to be excluded, left out and ignored. Some primary schools are doing this a part of their circle time or equivalent, and in secondaries that are experimenting with this, they are including it in the tutorial programmes, and evaluating it to see if it makes a difference to the calmness of lessons, the relationships between pupils, and their own self-reported indicators of inclusion. There will always be some for whom school is difficult, for a variety of complex reasons, whether from home or from experience, but for the majority it is possible to raise the sense of inclusion, of being part of a school if the ethic of everybody is talked about and attempts made to live up to it.

And what about the children themselves? Can they be encouraged to subscribe to the 'ethic of everyone' when there are no adults around, And indeed should they? Well, most children want to be happy and want those close to them to be happy. So by extension shouldn't they make a contribution to the inclusion of others if they want to be included themselves? So it is worth talking about who gets left out, what it was like when we were left out, because everyone has been at some point in their lives and if we see someone being left out, what can we do about it?

The 'ethic of everybody' needs to be considered not just in terms of inclusion for all, but a further dimension of contribution, otherwise we risk doing the ethics rather than expecting all to contribute. I am going to feel powerless if I am done to all the time, I am going to feel patronised and resentful. And eventually I will switch off. So sitting alongside the 'ethic of everybody' is that everybody makes a contribution. And that is something beyond the minimum, but relates instead to the unique gifts which someone can bring to this school, this classroom, this staffroom. If I'm a part of it I also want to be asked what I think, how I can make things better. Because it is through my contributions, the giving of advice and expertise that I become stronger, more confident and yes, hopeful rather than helpless.

Section Three
Aspects of hope in schools

18 Hopeful schools

'All I want is an education, and I am afraid of no one.'
Malala Yousafzai

Hopeful schools are about the ethos and atmosphere. They are settings where the school's aspirations are translated into action. In these places the school's mission statement and vision are expressed both symbolically and actually.

Highbury Grove School, for example, has aspirations which are expressed not only in words, but lived out in actions. The school has named each of the rooms after a significant contributor to the field of study taking place in that room[15]. 'The idea is to provide talking points around the school to help students think about their culture and history as well as to be inspired by human achievements in a wide range of disciplines. Some people are figures from history, some are still living; some are local people while others are key figures from around the world.'

Importantly, the naming of rooms is not confined solely to curriculum areas. So the staff base for student support is named after Thomas Coram who was a philanthropist who created the London Foundling Hospital to look after abandoned children in Lamb's Conduit Fields. And the nurture centre is named after Abraham Maslow. What is the impact of this? It is helping students and teachers to make a conscious connection between the subjects and areas they are engaged with, to see the bigger picture and wider horizons. This kind of thing encourages people, adults and young, to wonder what the connections might be and to be

---

15. highburygrove.islington.sch.uk/naming-our-classrooms/

intrigued to find out more. This sort of work costs nothing, but it has the impact of encouraging deeper thought. And at a personal level, to see the bigger landscape of the work they are doing and potentially to aspire to make a contribution on their own terms.

This 'naming' is signalling that the school is not an island, but rather is connected through time with big thinkers and contributors. It also has the potential to encourage colleagues to make the bigger connections with anything they are teaching. So, questions such as 'why is this important?' 'where does it fit into the bigger picture?' 'what is the history behind this?' 'what might our contribution be?'. It transforms the setting into one which has big, ambitious aspirations for all, and that includes teachers as well as students.

The second example is also via Highbury Grove. Its school motto is *'per ardua ad astra'* (through hard work to the stars) and the teaching and learning policy sets out its ambition that students need to feel they are on an adventure in the pursuit of wisdom:

'Plato talked about the need for philosopher kings; at Highbury Grove we wish to enable our pupils to become 'philosopher kids'. Philosopher kids are curious to know, question, and they can lead as well as follow. Philosopher kids like to feel, to think, and are notable for their eloquence and ability to take part in the 'great conversation' through which they make a contribution to our common life.

Philosopher kids engage thoughtfully in dialogue and argument, they appreciate and make beautiful things, they are confident when grappling with difficult ideas, they love music and also seek out space for quiet reflection and contemplation. We challenge all our pupils to become cultural polymaths, true 'renaissance people,' able to flourish both as individuals as well as realise that they have an important role to play in enabling their family, friends and community to flourish as well.'

How does the policy translate into being a 'hopeful school'? It sets out the scene for an ambitious, intellectually challenging diet which will create the space for children to become wise. This is ambitious and it doesn't happen overnight. People need to be brought on board. It echoes John Tomsett's[16] exceptionally high expectations for his year 7 students when engaging with Macbeth, using the same discipline and scholarship expected for A level studies. What it doesn't do is dumb down. And to get there, thoughtful leaders such as Tom Sherrington and John Tomsett take the time and trouble to put the groundwork in. First, by reading key texts which support the development of thinking about curriculum and assessment. Then, by asking colleagues what they make of it, leading sessions on aspects of the teaching and learning policy and the implications for classroom practice.

So, a big thread in developing hopeful schools is the opening up of horizons, not in a heavy handed way, but through gentle, powerful prompts which shift thinking higher, wider and deeper. And aligned with this are thoughtful conversations about making aspirations a reality.

The notion of a final product is evident in the examples above. Students were involved in the choosing of the eminent experts in the various curriculum areas; one of the expectations at Highbury Grove, for example is that all students have the chance to speak in public - either in the classroom on an aspect of their work, or in assemblies, or in wider fora such as public speaking competitions. None of this is easy. It takes practice, the willingness to take on feedback and being prepared to take the risk of potential embarrassment in public. But with encouragement, it is possible to be hopeful, rather than overcome by a feeling that it can't be done.

---

16. www.johntomsett.com/2016/08/27/this-much-i-know-about-unfettered-teaching/

There are other contexts doing this as well. School 21[17] where students work on projects which have a final audience, for example the school's exhibition of 'beautiful work'. The impact of the school providing such platforms is that students' efforts have a public forum where their work will be judged accordingly. This raises the game significantly and will produce many wobbly moments en route. But with support and the focus on the end product, these will be overcome. Hopefulness is a condition which paradoxically needs challenge and uncertainty to bring it to the fore. If everything were easy, there would be no sense of achievement. It is the hopefulness which provides the oil for the engine. In another example of work with an authentic audience, three Year 10 students from the school joined advertising group Ogilvy and Mather as interns and were given the brief of crafting a social media campaign for the London Village Network (LVN), aimed at deterring young people from getting involved with knife crime and inspiring them to make positive decisions for their future. At the heart of this is the ambition that pupils should have the opportunity to create things of genuine worth which have a genuine audience and purpose. Further examples of 'beautiful work'[18] for genuine audiences include writing and performing a play for primary children and advising local residents on sustaining wild habitats.

The examples from these schools show that through thinking about the curriculum and its wider story, they are providing students with opportunities to contribute, to grow and to feel hopeful rather than helpless.

17. www.school21.org.uk/
18. www.school21.org.uk/21st-century-approach/exhibitions-beautiful-work

19 Hopeful leaders

'A good leader takes a little more than his share of the blame, a little less than his share of the credit.'
Arnold Glasow

Amidst the fast-paced work of leaders in schools, there is one defining characteristic which seems to run through the work of the most effective. And this is that they have the capacity to find the glimmer of possibility of moving things forward, or of improvement in any situation. Now this is easy when things are going well, but it is a real test of character to keep this going when things are tough. What seems to happen is that these leaders are capable of stepping back, even if only for a few moments, to look for the potential for making things better.

In 'Don't Send Him in Tomorrow'[19] Jarlath O'Brien *'shines a light on the marginalised, disenfranchised and forgotten children of today's schools.'* While describing the provision for pupils with additional needs, he holds in absolute balance both the thoughtful practice of professionals in the sector and the considerable challenges they face. There are two significant aspects of hope which O'Brien articulates: the first is a call to all in mainstream settings to spend some time in a special school: to experience what is possible. And second, in describing the behaviour and attitude of one of his students, for whom a life of crime is considerably more appealing than knuckling down to something more worthy, he recognises that for all his best efforts and those of other professionals, this student is likely to be within the criminal justice system for much of his life. O'Brien's reflection on this is framed around a long-distance hope: he argues that if up to 60 per cent of those in prison have functional literacy below the age of five, then this is

---

19. www.amazon.co.uk/Dont-Send-Him-Tomorrow-disenfranchised/dp/1781352534

a call for arms for all professionals, to renew efforts for robust and humane teaching of reading and writing, particularly for those whom alternative means of 'employment' beckon. To pull this off at a national level will need industrial quantities of hope. But with professionals like Jarlath O'Brien making the case, it is likely that more will take note and act.

Critical to hope is that it doesn't seek to cast blame. It looks instead squarely at what has gone wrong and works to address it. The hopeful leader does not trade on the mistakes of the past, but rather sees the potential of the future. This is important, because hopeful leaders are big-spirited, they do not seek to enlarge their own reputations by comparing their work with what has gone before. They take the situation as it is, and see what needs to be done.

This is easier said than done, of course. But in the negotiating of the school to the trust, in reforming governance and leadership, in motivating the staff who remained, in bringing in new colleagues, it was hope that was the thread going through the work. Hopefulness engenders cheerfulness, and in being cheerful, the work is still hard but it is accompanied by an ease and grace that would not otherwise be there. Hope held things together. And it did so in tangible ways as well. The school's mission statement is one built on hope - on character, on opportunity and on human development, intellectual, physical and cultural. And those are not just words on the website and the banners. They are translated into the way that behaviour is managed, the way that lessons are planned and the way that additional opportunities are thought about.

Hopefulness cuts through complacency, because it is looking to the future. It is not self-centred, although it takes care of the self. This might sound contradictory, but hopefulness includes everyone, including the person exhibiting it, without it becoming a matter of exclusive self-concern. Where hopefulness is missing, people become depressed, the work is burdensome, people fear that their work is not taken seriously and it can seem rather pointless. However, it only takes one person to shift into a hopeful mode and it eventually spreads. In one school, leaders had become complacent and in spite of declining results, had attempted to lay these at the door of the students' backgrounds. There was a constant reference by leaders to the poverty of the local area, the lack of aspiration and a message of what can we do? There was no sense of taking stock of the reason for the declining results and acting on them. And all this was in a context of a school building which had had considerable millions spent on it, first-class facilities and beautifully landscaped grounds. Now, not that the physical surroundings necessarily have an impact on hopefulness, but nevertheless, the focus was on what was wrong relating to external factors, including the students' low prior attainment, rather than celebrating the great resources they already had.

However, in this school, there were a handful of staff who were not only hopeful, but were acting on that hope. It was evident from the work they were doing and the impact they were having, that strides were being made in their areas - of leading developments to support students from disadvantaged backgrounds, to the leadership of students with special educational needs, to the leadership of the sixth form. All were quietly doing great work and they knew they were making a difference. Their hopefulness shone in contrast to that of the leaders. Not that the leaders were cynical. But they were not looking through the lens of the possibility of hope and thinking about how things might be different and better, for instance considering how they could draw on the excellent practice evident in many parts of the school and to bring this to a wider audience. Without the hopeful lens, they were locked in the mindset of 'this is the way things are, we don't think we can do any better'.

20 Hopeful teachers

'I'm lucky I had some teachers who saw something in me.'
Ann Bancroft

Hopeful teachers are not all-singing, all dancing. Nor are they jazz handed as they go about their work. Instead, they have a quiet conviction that most things will go well, most of the time. This is not about expecting everything to go right all the time, because developing a hopeful professional disposition is not about perfection. Rather, it is about finding a thread through the messiness of every day transactions with young people that help to remind us that mostly, things are more positive than they are bad.

So how does this translate into practice? What does the hopeful teacher do? Well for a start, the environment is welcoming. It doesn't matter whether displays are intricate, elaborate, or not. But it matters that they send out the signal, that children's work and learning is valued. So, a bit of thought is put into them. They are not just there for show, they do not need to be perfect, but they do need to be used, and if not, changed. And, there might be a case for no displays at all. In some schools, walls have been deliberately stripped back, so that simplicity and clean space are used as deliberate messages. But this doesn't mean that they are not welcoming. The hopeful teacher has thought this through, and rather than laminating everything that moves, has taken deliberate action to think things through from the eyes of the learner. What is appropriate for this class, for this subject? Is there a case for fewer things which have more impact? And even if the displays are busy, again the hopeful teacher will have thought this through.

Then, the hopeful teacher has high expectations of behaviour because they know the difference between wishful thinking and hope. Wishful thinking expects things to happen well and to turn out for the best, but without the effort, and sometimes hard grind which goes into it. The hopeful teacher carefully thinks through what their expectations are for behaviour and conduct in the classroom. They start with their own list of expectations. The shorter and more succinct the better. Hopeful teachers share these with their classes and ask them whether they agree and whether they can suggest anything else to include, or anything which might be changed. In opening up the conversation to include everyone, the teacher still has the final say, but is ensuring a level of buy-in from pupils and students. The hope is forward looking, because when the behaviour expectations are not met, it is perfectly reasonable to say, 'but this is what we agreed'. This is where the graft of hope comes in: the work done to make things go more smoothly in the future.

There are times when either there is a particularly tricky group in secondary, or when things have not gone well in primary and it's hard to keep the hope going as far as behaviour is concerned. What some teachers have found helpful is to spend a few moments, literally a couple of minutes before the start of the lesson, imagining the youngsters in the best possible light. Doing all the things they are meant to be doing, cheerfully on task and without anyone mucking about. What seems to happen is that this imaginary scene in our heads translates into an unspoken expectation. And while this might need to be reinforced with a verbal expectation, what is happening is that we are projecting a version of the class as a whole and of individual characters as the best possible. If we work on the basis that children will 'catch' their attitudes from us, if we are sending out the message that they will be good, it quite often turns out that they are. And in keeping the good behaviour momentum going, these teachers will catch children doing the right thing, thus reinforcing their prior positive expectations, rather than getting into a downward spiral.

And so, the worst possible scenario, and it's happened to us all, when it has all gone wrong. Here, it is about how we recharge, not how we endure. It is important to sound out another colleague, get advice and support, physical if necessary. Not to police the classroom, but to provide a coherent message about expectations. But what is essential here is that once expectations have been made clear again and once the turf has been re-laid, that the past is the past. That it is literally and metaphorically a fresh start. Hopeful teachers realise that however badly things have gone, most children are not setting out to do a rubbish job. They mostly want to do well, partly for its own satisfaction, partly to please us as teachers and parents at home. And the hopeful teacher taps into that deeper motivation and reminds themselves they are starting again. Each day is a new day.

Part of the agenda of the hopeful teacher is to feed the well that reminds them why they do the job, beyond the job. That the pleasure of being with young people feeds them as professionals as well. So they enjoy their company, enjoy their stories and their jokes, and in so doing, build their reservoirs of hope. And these reservoirs are enjoyed for their own sake and are a deep resource for when things go wrong.

21 Hopeful children

'Let us remember: One book, one pen, one child, and one teacher can change the world.

Malala Yousafzai

Children are naturally hopeful. For most of them, the slings and arrows of life have not yet discouraged them. Most of them are curious, want to learn and want to please their teachers and parents. Their curiosity about themselves, about the world around them and their peers is a sign that they are naturally hopeful. However, it is easy for this light to be diminished. This can be done by careless talk such as comparing them with siblings or with other children in the class, by labelling them, by pouring scorn on their efforts, their speech or their best efforts. This is not necessarily done intentionally, but it has the effect of reducing their hope about how well they are doing and what they might achieve in the future.

There are three aspects to this - the first is that adults need to let children know, through their words and the way they treat them, that they are unique, that they have a contribution to make to the classroom and to their peers, just by their presence. The second is that they all have something to offer. And the third is that they can all get better, because we can all get better.

So, how do we show children that we appreciate them for the uniqueness that they bring to a classroom? One way is by providing them with opportunities to talk about the things they are interested in, both in lessons and outside of school. Some schools are using 'Genius Hour' to create opportunities for children to work on something which holds their interest and which they can develop and research further. Through this, adults are able to see what motivates a child and through the things they produce during the Genius Hour[20] are able to show their expertise. By encouraging this development of expertise, adults are showing children that they have unique insights into their research projects and that this is worth talking about and sharing with others. Through this work, children of whatever prior attainment, see themselves as researchers and experts in things and are more knowledgeable about these than their peers and teachers. This is not to set up the idea of being big headed but rather a deep, quiet pride in personal work and achievements.

The benefits of this spill over into formal classwork. There will be times when the work is hard. It should be, because otherwise learning is not taking place. But with the knowledge that they are good at their particular interest, they can be encouraged to transfer this over to keep persevering with other tasks they find demanding. It acts as a kind of inoculation against the difficulties which everyone faces, and provides resilience in the face of these.

The second way to embed children's sense of hopefulness is to encourage them to see that they have something to offer. One of the most powerful ways we can build someone's self-confidence is to ask them for their advice. This might sound counter-intuitive in a classroom, because the teacher does not naturally ask children for advice. But some schools are experimenting with this. They are asking things like, 'We have a problem with some children being unkind to others at playtime. What would you do?' 'I'm not sure whether the display works better this way, or that. What do you think?' Or they are reading stories which contain a dilemma and they say, 'Well, I'm not sure what the right course of action would be here. What do you think?' The fact of asking 'What do you think?' means that children see themselves as capable of having an opinion, which is taken seriously by an adult. Children see themselves as people with ideas to contribute. And when this happens, they are likely to do more.

---

20. www.geniushour.com

Some schools are doing this, even with very young children. For example, in deciding which trip a class of five-year-olds should make, they set up a table with pictures of the options on them. In front of each was a bowl and as children decided where they would like to go, they placed a pebble in to the bowl of their choice. In doing this, the children were being asked to make a decision, and were being sent a powerful message that their views count. This was extended further by the children being asked to give their reasons for their choice. This kind of activity supports children in thinking that their views count, that they can make a contribution and this supports their sense of hopefulness about what they might achieve.

In some secondary schools where teachers have realised the power of involving students by drawing on their help and expertise, many schools ask older students to mentor younger ones or support with reading, or invite sixth formers to share their thoughts on what they wished they had focused on at key stage four. What these schools have found is that students not only rise to the challenge, but they are eager to do more. They see themselves as being contributors rather than just consumers. And this has been found to be particularly effective when students are demotivated or regularly in trouble in school. By asking them whether they can help with this, they are being treated with respect, with ideas and views of their own. And in this subtle way are more hopeful about what they might achieve in school.

22 Hopeful classrooms

'The more that you read, the more things you will know.
The more that you learn, the more places you'll go.'
Dr Seuss

John Tomsett has written about how much he enjoys teaching Year 7 students English. They have been studying Macbeth. In one post[21] he says something very striking *'I have ignored any inherited assessment data about the students and instead I have taught relentlessly to the very top, expecting that everyone in the class can write literary analysis of the Scottish Play. It has been liberating.'* Why might ignoring students' prior attainment be an indicator of 'hopeful' rather than 'helpless'? Essentially, because he is not putting any limits on children's potential, based on their prior attainment. And this wilful ignorance has produced some interesting results.

By making the assumption that everyone in his class, with the right support, can access the play, that they will enjoy it and that they will produce high quality work, he is setting the implicit platform of hopefulness. And there is absolutely no dumbing down. The text is key. They start most lessons by reciting the first scene, by heart. That's it, by heart. So the expectation is that every child and he, as the teacher, will have learnt it. And interestingly, he describes it as 'fun'. And that's because difficult things, mastered and shared aloud are enjoyable. This is not a one-off gimmick, but a deep resource which is being built, which is developing children's love of language and a deep pride in their grappling with it through memorising it.

---

21. www.johntomsett.com/2016/08/27/this-much-i-know-about-unfettered-teaching/

He then goes on to say that he sometimes shares extracts from the latest book he is writing. This is showing his vulnerability as a creative author, honouring the students' observations on his work. And paradoxically, by sharing work in progress and asking for their feedback, modelling how to be hopeful. As a result, some of his students have been sharing their own creative writing, and the class is on its way to creating its own blog to share their work, and that includes John's. A shared endeavour. Teacher and students making sense of Macbeth and as a parallel endeavour, writing their own material resulting in a vibrant, deep spirit of scholarship and creativity.

Given this place of high expectation, coupled with significant enjoyment, John found that his students were identifying themes such as 'fair is foul and foul is fair' as they went through the play, which he had not noticed before. Now, when a teacher finds that students are gleaning insights which he or she had not noticed before, and they acknowledge this, something very powerful happens. In letting students know that they have contributed to the teacher's learning and understanding of a text, in this example, it strengthens their own agency The narrative goes something like this: 'Boy, if the teacher hadn't spotted this and they are delighted with my making the connection, I bet I can find more.' The onus of learning, when this happens, shifts from extrinsic (doing something either for the grade or to please a teacher) to the internal. And it is the internal where scholarship, a deep engagement with the material, takes place.

'One of the things I explained to the whole class is that there is no point me setting them work they find easy. I have to challenge them with activities beyond their current capacity, teach them well and believe, without a shred of doubt, that they can meet the challenge.' And, true to his word, he sets them the same structure for writing their essays, as he would an A level group. They are shown how to back up their commentary with quotes from the play and to engage with the effect which Shakespeare is having on his audience. What he is delighted to find is that they are capable of doing this. And

in the process, they come up with their own incisive observations of the text. Parallel to this, they are developing their own work as creative writers. And not just the high prior attainers. John shares an example of one student, for whom writing does not come naturally, which shows his critical engagement with the text and his own unique insights into it. And it emerges that this student is also writing in his own time and preparing a short story for the class blog.

When it comes to parents' evening, John finds that they are all saying how much their children are enjoying the lessons on Macbeth; that many of them are reciting passages at home and are talking about what they have learnt. The bedrock of trust, established in the classroom, has spilled out into the children's wider lives, affecting their parents and siblings. John didn't necessarily set out to align his work as 'hopeful', but the impact of his absolute focus on high expectations, shared endeavour and the opening up of immense possibilities, has done this. And all because of Macbeth and a refusal to dumb down.

So what might be the implications of this for wider school practice? Might it be worth asking - what is the highest we can expect our children to achieve? With the expectation that they will not get it straight away - why would they, because it is meant to be demanding. Are there implications beyond this example in English? Some schools are providing this additional challenge by encouraging children to read about the lives of significant figures in other curriculum areas. So, in maths for example, some are researching the life of Fibonnacci, or finding out about Fermi's questions and sharing these with the class. In RE, some are collecting examples of religious belief, practice and abuse from the news and making the connections with what they are learning in class. And there are fabulous examples in art and design technology, where the exploration of the lives, techniques and impact of the giants in their field, are opening up new vistas for children. And in the process, supporting them to feel hopeful, not helpless.

23 Hopeful governors

'The quality of a leader is reflected in the standards they set for themselves.'

Ray Kroc

The strongest governing bodies express hope for their schools. Governance is demanding and complicated and the balance between challenge and support is not straightforward. These are some of the characteristics of hopeful governors: they know the school well, they understand information and data, they connect with the local community, they bring their wider experience and wisdom to the school, they support the big events, they make time to visit the school on a normal day, they notice the good things going on and they provide support, without being soft, to the head and senior leaders, they keep track of the budget, ensuring value for money, they ensure there is a succession plan in place, both for the governing body and for the school leaders. And above all they support leaders in developing and expressing a shared vision for the school.

To take each of these in turn. In knowing the school, they understand its long and recent history, the trials and difficulties as well as the successes. They remember to take the long view, putting any personal interests aside, when holding the school to account - they might say for example 'look at what has been achieved in the last few years' or 'the school still needs to develop this, what's the best way to go about it?' They understand the importance of supporting people where they are and helping them get to where they need to be. They know that very few people set out to do the wrong thing and take this into account when in conversation with school colleagues. Above all they are humane. They join in the celebrations and work collegiately when things need to improve.

Hopeful governors make sure that their governance skills are up to date. The role is an increasingly complex one and it is important that they keep themselves informed: on interpreting data, on the complexities of financial governance, on personnel. They do this either by attending courses run by the local authority, within their MAT (multi-academy trust) and if none are available, they organise their own. By investing in growing their expertise they are expressing hope for the school. And each member of the governing body or trust will have their own expertise, which they are happy to share with others.

In supporting the big events as well as visits during the normal school day, they are affirming the school's work and providing a great audience for pupils to show what they are able to do. So by attending events, they communicate their commitment to all in the school. And they remember to thank all staff, including those who keep the school clean, serve lunches and greet people when they arrive at the school. These gestures send important messages of purpose and hope to all in the community.

And they know how well the children at the school are doing. They know how much the budget is, how much comes into the school as additional funding for children from disadvantaged backgrounds. They ask questions about how the money is spent and the impact it has had on pupils' achievement. And if outcomes for the pupils are not improving, they suggest alternative paths to research such as through the Education Endowment Foundation, consider the Pupil Premium awards or contact schools who are doing well in this area.

Many governors gain insight to the work of the school by running pupil panels. With a sample of children from different backgrounds, they tease out what the school is doing well and report this back to the head and senior leaders; they ask what might make the school better; whether they are happy to come to school, whether they would recommend it to a friend moving to the area; whether teachers give them work which makes them think and work hard; whether teachers help them to improve, whether they feel safe, what happens if anyone is bullied etc.

It is not necessary for every member of the governing body or trustee to do everything - the wide range of responsibilities should be shared. Then the summaries of what has been found shared with others.

And school leaders need to express gratitude to those who give up their time and offer their expertise, for no remuneration. When these relationships are honest and healthy, schools really fly.

24 Look how far we've come

'I was set free because my greatest fear had been realised, and I still had a daughter who I adored, and I had an old typewriter and a big idea. And so rock bottom became a solid foundation on which I rebuilt my life.'

J K Rowling

There are times when being hopeful is more of an aspiration than a reality. In which case it is important to restore the reservoir. And one way of doing this is to take a few moments to remind ourselves of just how far we have come. In a professional life, that will have meant being trained, doing years of study, practising. And wherever we are on the professional stages, whether newly qualified, recently qualified or experienced and mature, the journey is still one which is worth reflecting on.

In looking back at the progress any of us had made, small gains, taken every day, these are cumulative over the years. The problem is that we don't spend enough time looking back to see what a body of effort and work we have behind us. And when we do, we realise that it is possible to be hopeful again for the future.

The fragile hold which we sometimes feel about our own competence can undermine our efforts to be positive about what we have to face today, let alone any big work for the future. Every day can seem like a struggle. So, what some colleagues do, is to take time at the beginning of a new term, to look back at what they have done with their classes the previous term. With the distance of a few weeks this can often be seen with greater clarity. And they jot down a few of these. The list does not need to be exhaustive, but it does need a few moments to reflect on them. And then to say, 'Well done us'. This is not done in a spirit of pride or of complacency, but rather to look fairly and squarely at just how much has been covered: the number of books which children have read, the new understanding in maths, the pieces of extended writing. All these have been done with the teacher's work, support and guidance. And this is no mean feat.

Then looking beyond the classroom practice, to think about the help offered to others; the contribution to a staff meeting, the presentation at a TeachMeet, these are things which should be quietly reflected on, from a distance, so that they deepen our reserves for being hopeful for what is possible in the future.

Wise leaders know that it is important for a school to do this as a whole. At the start of a new academic year, there are reviews of the achievements and the areas for development for the new year. These need to be held in equal balance. While it is important to get a grip on what needs to move forward and to improve, it is also essential to pay tribute to the gains as well. And to thank people for their efforts, not just in a generic sense, but by giving examples of just how far the school collectively, and the professionals within it, have come. Some schools at the beginning of the academic year have an all-inclusive meeting with *all* staff where there is a discussion about the whole school ethos and the value of every individual. Not a top-down talk from the SLT, but a meaningful discussion resulting in action points which will be taken forward and developed. If the whole school ethos is revisited every year, so that everyone feels included in the vision and the ongoing journey, then people will feel valued and more motivated. And that particularly so, if after the results, some departments are not as good as hoped for, but that they feel supported instead of damned. Brief examples of children's successes, both in actual results and also in progress from their starting points, growth in confidence, a brief overview of what is in place now which wasn't there before, will pay sufficient tribute to the notion of 'look how far we've come.' Some schools have a board in the staffroom and colleagues are encouraged to contribute their own comments on 'look how far we've come'. This is kept fresh and organic, for example through the use of post-its. And in some cases it is a standing item on a staff meeting agenda. It only takes a few minutes, but it is like a shot of energy when people are tired, and there is still more to do.

This capturing of the small gains is essential in coming to understand just how much has been achieved. Daily living and working seems to flow as though these are just ephemera when in fact they are coalescing over time into significant achievements.

This applies not just to adults as professionals but also to children in the classroom. At the heart of assessment for learning, are high quality conversations about what has gone well and what else might need to be done to improve it. So, the capturing of 'look how far I've come' is an important aspect of a child's learning. In many schools, children are encouraged to look back over their work and to register for themselves just what they can do now, compared with a week ago, a term ago, a year ago. This kind of review not only makes the learning more secure, but also gives the child more reason to be hopeful, when they tackle difficult things in the future. It is in making the implicit explicit that provides the basis for being hopeful about demanding work in the future. If I could do this before, I can do it in the future.

One way of capturing children's confidence and growth in confidence, which is closely related to being hopeful, is to get them to capture their attitudes at the start of a new term, or a new piece of work. How confident are they about starting a new class, or beginning to do an extended piece of writing, or tackle some really hard problems in maths? Some schools use tools like the Blob Tree[22] to do this with children working individually, in pairs, or as a whole class, the tree is then shared and discussed. Where are we on the tree? Why is that? It is ok to feel nervous and uncertain about new classes, new work? The Blob Trees are dated. Then they are returned to a while later. This could be as short as later that day, a week or even a term later. And the children are

---

22. www.blobtree.com/

asked the same question - where are you now on the tree? And by and large, their identification of the blobs show that they are feeling better or more confident. But instead of this being invisible and unstated, it is brought to the fore and talked about. And in talking about it, the sense of the journey in confidence becomes concrete. Children recognise just how far they've come. And this feeds their hope for the future.

25 Embracing obstacles

'Obstacles, of course, are developmentally necessary: they teach kids strategy, patience, critical thinking, resilience and resourcefulness.'
Naomi Wolf

When Vic Goddard agreed to the television crews coming in to his school, I'm sure he knew he was taking a risk. And some of it must have been pretty hairy. But what great stories emerged from the series. The story which swept everyone away was the boy who joined the school in Year 9. He had been living abroad and his mother was keen to ensure that she found a school where he would be accepted and where his needs would be met. His needs were complex but what was interesting was that neither his mother nor the school defined him by these.

What the film showed was how he was able to rise to the occasion, and a very big one, to talk to his peers at the end of his school days about what it had meant to be a student in that school. Not only in terms of his academic work, but in terms of how he had developed as a human being and the growth in his confidence. The school had provided him with opportunities to grow and the evidence for this was seen in his speech to his peers at the final year 11 assembly.

And the end result was that he was able to show himself as the magnificent human being he is. And most importantly captured the spirit of the school and showed a way for others to do the same. He was allowed to be himself.

The school through its quiet, understated support had created the conditions for him to be hopeful and most importantly the space to exhibit the results of that hope. They had faith in him. This was far removed from a deficit model of what cannot be done, and was rather a case of what can and might be done.

Young people with additional needs are often seen as needing interventions. And this is quite right, when they need additional support to catch up with their classmates. Schools do good work when they identify what might be some of the barriers to learning and work to overcome these. However, they are missing a trick if they don't look beyond this and ask themselves and the pupil well what might be possible? What would really stretch them? What could they do on their own terms? This shifts the agenda from 'being done to', even if this is well done, and opens the conversations up to 'what else is possible?' or 'what can you bring to the party?'. And that is exactly what happened in Ryan's case in 'Educating Essex'.

Some schools ensure that they take account of the things which a child does outside of school, often in situations where they are excelling or have great knowledge. There are some children who are excelling in sport, fishing and drama beyond the school day. Some are helping to care for younger siblings, others are brilliant cooks. In having conversations about these, the agenda is opened up to link the things they are good at, to the potential for developing these skills in school. Not that it is about bringing these into the curriculum, but it is about showing them that they have expertise and knowledge in one area and can think about how they achieved that. And then think about how they might translate that into thinking about their work in school.

There was one student who was a champion kick boxer. His work in school was slapdash and his attitude to learning less than positive. But when the school found out about his achievements outside school, they asked him to share what he did, how he practised, how he had achieved what he had done, with other students. He got on stage and spoke to them. His pride in his high quality work elsewhere was the trigger for him realising that he could translate this into his application to his schoolwork. What the school had done was to honour his achievements, given him a platform to talk about these and were able to show him through this opportunity that he could do the same in school. Hopefulness in one context was translated into another. Whilst he did not become a model student, he certainly shifted his focus from mucking about, to one of application. Most of the time.

The point about obstacles providing fertile ground for hope is taken seriously in some contexts. The thinking here is that pupils are capable of engaging with difficult stuff. One school for example, asks groups of pupils to act as improvement partners. Alongside the formal school improvement protocols, these pupils are asked to engage with aspects of school improvement, to discuss their contribution and to offer their ideas to senior leaders. Rather than seeing pupils as purely on the receiving end of school improvement work, they ask them to engage with it. And at Wellington College, Carl Hendrick manages a team of internally appointed research fellows who meet once a fortnight to discuss key literature and co-design surveys. He has also set up a student research council who meet every two weeks and who read the same literature that staff read and help co-design research tools. These two teams are not only advisory in nature but also ambassadorial.

26 Room 13

'Man needs, for his happiness, not only the enjoyment of this or that, but hope and enterprise and change.'
Bertrand Russell

If we take the view that by creating an atmosphere of hope rather than helplessness, it follows that pupils need opportunities to show their unique spirit. This means opportunities to show what they can do rather than what they can't. This is not about a free for all, aimless, self indulgent opportunity for self expression. It is instead a disciplined approach to the expectation that all make a contribution.

One example of this is Room 13 which started in Scotland in 1994, when a group of pupils established their own art studio in Room 13 in Caol Primary School near Fort William, Scotland. Like many things it was not planned, rather it emerged from an existing piece of work. In this case, the artist Rob Fairley began working with pupils. This meant that they were learning from a master, an expert who both showed them what was possible and created the balance of challenge and support for pupils to produce original work. When the project was over, the pupils were keen to continue. But funds had run out. However, rather than that being the end of it, the headteacher told the pupils that they could use a spare room in the school to continue the work. However, they wanted to have the same access to the high quality materials, the expertise and the knowledge of professional artists in the future. So they were given a small amount of money and told they could work out what to do.

What happened was that they organised themselves into a committee, started fund-raising, made contact with local art galleries and museums, invited experts in, created their work and most importantly generated income. While making money was not the main purpose, it was nevertheless essential for ensuring that the project continued. But the money followed the work. The reaching out to the wider art community, the participation in local art events, the engagement with professional artists, meant that their work attracted attention. And the sales and commissions followed.

What is interesting here is that the school leaders did not do this for them. What they did do was to create the opportunity for it to happen, kept an overview of health and safety both in terms of the physical space and in terms of the pupils making contact with adults from beyond the school. What they didn't do was micro-manage the process so that pupils were able to organise things as they saw fit, make mistakes and learn from them. However, beyond the health and safety, pupils also knew that they could ask adults for advice and support if they needed it.

The result of this piece of work meant that pupils in this school had reason to be hopeful rather than helpless. The involvement in a project which was bigger than themselves, which needed collective involvement and which required them to make contact with adults beyond the school, resulted in real ownership of a real project. Not some airy-fairy, feel-good token gesture, but one which had real inherent worth. Many of the pupils went on to work in the art world and all would have learnt deep lessons of getting involved and doing something which went beyond the school walls. Their project attracted international attention.

Now what was interesting here was that it was not set up as another 'nice' thing to do. The pupils had already had a good experience working with a professional artist. However, the wise headteacher provided them with a safe space to take their idea to the next stage. It was not forced on them, rather it was generated by them. There was no expectation that anything would come of it. There was however, a level of trust invested in the pupils - that they wouldn't spoil the room, that it was a privilege to have access to it and that they would make best use of it. Beyond that it was up to them.

And the process would not have been hunky dory. There would have been times when plans went wrong, when work was not as good as it might have been, when arrangements went awry. But because the children were working on something that was bigger than themselves, that needed collective effort, they persevered. There is something going on here which is to do with adults not over-planning every aspect of children's lives. Something going on which says 'let them have a go, what is the worst that can happen?'. The school provided just enough resources as seed corn, a little outlay and the materials at hand. It is unlikely that the headteacher foresaw the impact these understated gestures would have.

Room 13 is an example of how it is possible to release children's energy and enterprise. It spawned plenty of similar projects in other schools. And it is fair to say that while many of the children involved in the early projects have gone on to have careers in art and curation in art galleries, that was not the main point or intended outcome. The paradox is that there was no intended outcome. It emerged through trial and error. The work has spread with more than 80 settings across the world adopting the principles of Room 13. These new projects are still working to these principles. It is possible that the reason for this is that it takes a particular mindset of discipline and structure on the part of leaders to allow this to happen. Where it becomes micro-managed or constrained, it probably withers. This is speculation. But while that might be the case for Room 13, there are still messages to take from this work: that children have good ideas and that these can often lead to big enterprises. And the principle of running with children's ideas has the capacity for creating hope through ambitious enterprises.

Section 4
Developing hope

27 Today is not tomorrow

'Nobody, ever once, pops to the top. You walk there. Step by step, each a failure until it's not.'
Seth Godin

Seth Godin is a thinker who delves in to the deepest aspects of human motivation, purpose and success. The quote that nobody pops to the top is from a post Seth wrote about Van Gogh. He shows a picture of Ramsgate which the painter did when he spent time in England in the 1870's early in his career. Van Gogh's paintings of Ramsgate are fine. They are functional and recognisably Ramsgate. But they are not high art, nor do they point to Van Gogh's future wild, magnificent brilliance. What, asks Godin, would have happened if the painter had stopped painting in Ramsgate? What if he decided he wasn't that great a painter? Well, the answer is obvious. The Ramsgate paintings were a staging post on the journey to brilliance.

What Van Gogh was doing in Ramsgate was fine-tuning his craft. And the outcomes were perfectly competent. But they were like a thousand other mundane representations of British seaside towns. In practising at Ramsgate, he was training his eye, listening to the landscape and letting the process filter through the system of his artistic toolbox. The craft of every day work is what leads us to the potential for brilliant new insights down the road. That's the point; it will be in the future, not necessarily today. So in keeping the craft going, finely tuned, day-by-day, is the stuff of being hopeful, not helpless. Now, the analogy with Van Gogh can only go so far because of course, his life ended tragically. But it is possible to argue that in the process of creating the Ramsgate paintings and others, it was the seedbed, grounded in hope, which led to the subsequent brilliance.

How does the Ramsgate story translate into thinking about leadership? It's about recognising that the fairly mundane stuff of today, is sowing the seeds for a brilliant tomorrow. The routines, the boring stuff, become the raw material from which great things can emerge. It is simply not possible to do it without these. So wise leaders talk about how the daily practices of good, solid work, which lead to big outcomes. The two need to be held in mind at the same time. If we are only concentrating on the Ramsgate experience then we can become disheartened. Because frankly a lot of day-to-day stuff is routine. But the power comes when these routines are linked to and meshed to a bigger picture. One of greatness, of high outcomes, of a hopeful, better future. However, there are no quick fixes and wise leaders know this. They do the right thing day by day and fire up the energy levels and imagination both for themselves and those they are working with by drawing on the bigger picture for where this work is heading. They paint the story of the journey from Ramsgate to the Auvergne, from the soggy seaside to the sunflowers.

And for children in the classroom, these metaphors hold true too. The Ramsgate paintings are the times tables, the spellings, the grammar, the rules of any subject area which must be mastered. They are the vital ingredients from which magnificent stuff can be made. But if children are only locked into the grammar, spelling, times tables without seeing where this might lead, then that is a pity. It is more than a pity as it can lead to feeling hopeless. It shifts from a depressing story to an inspiring story when children see the equivalent of the journey which Van Gogh made, figuratively, from his Ramsgate period to the sunflowers.

The metrics of spelling, punctuation and grammar are the essentials for going on to do great stuff.

This is not to argue that we will all be aiming to produce work of the quality of Van Gogh. But it is to make the case that what appears pedestrian today, can open up new avenues for the future. However, they will not be opened up without doing the boring stuff first. In fact, it is only boring when we don't see the point. Which is the point of using analogies like the Ramsgate painting. Most of us are prepared to keep going with something if we can see where it might lead, if we can imagine where it might go and if we can have some inkling of the journey on route. However, it is hard to persevere when there is no wider landscape into which to sketch our efforts.

There are similarities here with Austin's Butterfly[24]. When Ron Berger worked with two groups of students analysing how Austin might improve his original attempt at drawing a butterfly, they were participating in the equivalent of a Ramsgate process: namely, moving from the here and now to the future. They discussed the process of thinking about and providing feedback. They talked about how it is important to be specific, precise and kind. In doing so, they were developing their own self regulation as well as analysing the work in hand. What Berger was able to show the children, was that the basics of any work can and should be improved. But that this will only happen when the conditions are both challenging and kind. 'We were not mean about it' said one of the children, when reflecting on the quality of the feedback they had given. In working with the children in this way, Berger was showing them how to be hopeful, not helpless about improving not just this piece of work, but any piece of work. There is also something here about trust: Austin was prepared and willing to trust the judgement of those who suggested improvements. This was because they were considering his best interests, that they had faith and confidence in him, that with their guidance, he could make improvements.

---

24. www.vimeo.com/38247060

And that this work takes place, step by step, with plenty of mistakes on the way. But mostly these are not life-threatening, so we can live with them. Because it's one of the principles of being hopeful, not helpless. That our work can always be better.

28 Perfection and aspiration

'The artist who aims at perfection in everything achieves it in nothing.'
Eugene Delacroix

One of the biggest mistakes we can make is to think that we have got to be perfect. There is no such thing as perfection in this world. We make ourselves miserable and also less productive when we try to be perfect. The world has good and bad things in it, in equal measure. For the most part there is nothing we can do about things which are beyond our control. What we can do though, is to reflect on those things which are within our control and choose to do two things: first, to hold a very clear-sighted view about the world as it actually is - the good and the bad, the beautiful and the ugly. And the second is to maintain a clear view about what is realistic to improve both in our lives and our work.

This is a balancing act. And like all balancing acts it is likely to go one way or the other unless we pay attention. There are times when the balance tips over into the negative and there are times when we beat ourselves up for not getting things right. But that is ok. It is in the finding of the balance that the marginal gains, day by day, start building over time and add considerable value to our work over time.

Let us consider first why perfection is unhelpful and yet why we beat ourselves up for not achieving it. There used to be a saying in Fleet Street that as a young journalist, you could either create a perfectly crafted piece of work and miss the deadline, or you could meet the deadline with something that was very good, just not perfect. The deadline always trumps. The pursuit of perfection does not support the agenda of being hopeful, not helpless. In fact, it can create the opposite. By setting ourselves standards which are too high, and therefore very unlikely that we are going to reach those standards, we can become defeated and despondent and give up as a result.

The second problem with perfection is that it can make life difficult for those around us, both at home and at work. If we are pursuing unrealistic goals and it is making us miserable and snappy because they are unlikely to be achieved, then we are probably spreading a helpless rather than hopeful vibe. At work, this can mean that targets are set are very unlikely to be reached. This is different from setting the 'big, hairy, audacious goals' pioneered by Jim Collins and which are aspirational and exciting. In setting targets which are too high, they are not aspirational and exciting and when these are not met, there is likely to be a loss of confidence. The targets need to be realistic and based on where we are now. Wise leaders understand this. They work with people where they are, not where they want them to be. And they understand that not only is perfection not possible, it is only through incremental steps that we are going to get sustainable improvements.

There is a big difference though when we consider aspiration. The root of the word, the etymology of aspiration comes from the Latin 'to breathe or breathe upon'. It is a kinder, more realistic place to be and it also holds out the promise for us to reach our highest potential. It is different from the perfection agenda in three main respects - first, that aspiration is grounded in the reality of here and now; second it is hopeful rather than helpless when we have setbacks; and third it is more flexible than perfection - it is an image, often a concrete image, of where we might reasonably be. And the paradox is that when aspirations are high, humane and honest, they are more likely to be reached than an uncompromising perfect standard.

So how do leaders talk aspiration rather than perfection? They talk about how things might be and how the journey might look to get there. They articulate a clear picture both for their own growth and also for the school. They are able to take both the long and the short view: 'This is what I am working towards - these are the things I hope to see next week, next month, next year. And this is what I am going to do about it today.' These are hopeful ways of thinking and talking about the future. The more realistic aspiration allows for a picture of future richness and also expresses enjoyment of the journey en route. This means embracing the stuff that goes wrong, as triggers for new learning, rather than prompts for giving up.

These leaders talk about the potential they see in others - and they do this in a way which is honest, not patronising, but full of sincerity. And it is always grounded in what that person has already done. So that they can see the link between where they are now and where they might be. 'You are exceptionally good at x, y and z, have you thought where this might go?' This articulation of the world as it is and the world as it might be taps into our deepest need for growth and for our capacity to be better. And this way of working is grounded in the goodness of the here and now, not on some unrealistic jump into a magical future.

What then follows is that teachers in classrooms do the same. They affirm what children are already doing well and they talk about how this could be bigger, better, bolder tomorrow. And this is possible, because pupils are already doing some of it now; they are sowing the seeds for better outcomes in the future. And the hopeful agenda provides the water for those seeds to grow into something magnificent. And this is at the heart of being hopeful, not helpless.

29 On achieving with little

'It is amazing what you can accomplish if you do not care who gets the credit.'

Harry S Truman

One of the triggers for feeling helpless is a sense that we do not have the resources or the capacity to do what we want to do. Often, this is tied up with physical resources and money. The narrative goes like this: well, if I had such and such, it would be fine. But I don't, so it's very unlikely to happen. And that is the end of the story. Except that it needn't be. The feelings of frustration are natural and they should be acknowledged, but they should not necessarily be the end point. Often, not always, there is a way through.

It is helpful to notice examples, when they come our way, of people who have done something with very little, when the odds seemed stacked against them. These serve as a reminder that often it is possible to do something positive even when the tide seems to be against us. The BBC's Food and Farming Awards are a striking example of these. A community in the Forest of Dean, which did not have sufficient population density to support a local market, thought laterally and set up a virtual market.[25] This is a forum for local suppliers to showcase their produce and for local people to be able to buy it. What was surprising was that until this project was up and running, many people had no idea that there was, for instance, a coffee-roasting business in their locality, or that so much great food was being grown locally. Now the point here is not about the availability of coffee, but the process by which the platform came into existence. Instead of saying, well there are too few people to make a market viable, the thinking was, well what else can we do to make this happen if we think it is important? The

---

25. www.bbc.co.uk/programmes/profiles/491yPKgFBkbhVkBJzp95sR8/best-food-market www.deanforestfoodhub.org.uk

'if it is important' is crucial, because when things don't immediately fall into place, there might be good reasons for it. And the barriers might serve to realise that we would be wasting our time. So barriers can be helpful. But, if we believe something is important, then we start to think creatively about how we might get there. What is interesting about the Forest of Dean example, is that in trying to emulate the traditional food fairs and markets, brilliant as these often are, and realising that it would not be possible, they imagined something else which not only serves the people in allowing local produce to be available, it also fulfils some of the ways in which markets are about people. Because the produce is delivered through local pubs, local shops, churches and even schools. So, from a deficit model, this example has shown that it is possible to bring people and products together. And in doing so, they are providing a way for other rural, sparsely populated areas to do the same.

There are in fact benefits to not immediately having the resources available. When everything is ready for what we need two things often happen: we can sometimes be wasteful, because we do not put as much value on something which is to hand and which we haven't had to make an effort to procure. The second thing that can happen is that we are not as imaginative as we might be if things are too easy. Why would we try out new ways and see if things might be better with less, if we don't have to? Another example from the Food and Farming Awards: in Kilburn in London, Dee Woods[26] was determined to do something about the fact that people are going hungry. Noticing that a building had been empty for seven years she persuaded the authorities to let her have it and twice a week cooks food for anyone who turns up, at no charge. How does she do it? Well, in having the imagination first to see that in this day and age there are still people going hungry and second, realising that there was something she could do about it. And it is not some bland offering either, but the brilliant use of herbs and spices to create magic and in teaching others how to do the same, with very little. Similarly, 'A Girl called Jack' and the 9p burger.[27] Not created out of a need to be clever, but out of necessity.

---

26. www.southkilburnnw6.london/news-blog/granville-community-kitchen-s-dee-woods-wins-bbc-cook-of-the-year

How does this translate into schools? A recognition that while great buildings and resources are desirable, they are not necessary. That where money is spent, it is spent on the highest quality materials for children. For example, in one school's early years classroom, the children use artist quality crayons. Why not the cheapest one? Because the thinking was that children's work should be treated with respect and that the investment in high quality materials would send a strong signal to them that their work is important.

Sitting behind this is the idea that we work with people and resources where we are, not where we would like to be. A deep understanding that people are more capable than they realise and that it is possible to do much with little.

What happens if we set out to achieve with less in the classroom? By thinking through deliberately limiting what we give to our pupils, by asking them how they might make something go further, by telling them that if everything were easy, we would not exercise our muscles and so become stronger. To give them a project with very little funding and ask them to work out what they can do. Is it worthwhile, is it going to add value, and so what can they do, with very little. And afterwards, what have they learnt.

---

27. www.cookingonabootstrap.com/2015/01/31/carrot-cumin-kidney-bean-burger-9p/

30 Courage can be contagious

'You may not always have a comfortable life and you will not always be able to solve all of the world's problems at once but don't ever underestimate the importance you can have because history has shown us that courage can be contagious and hope can take on a life of its own.

Michelle Obama

Courage can be contagious - what does this mean? Courage is the deep personal bravery which comes from facing difficulties fairly and squarely. It is not about not feeling the fear, but it is about acknowledging it and refusing to be cowed. All life is tough. There are times when it is overwhelmingly so, but when we refuse to bow out, we are exhibiting courage. It is the refusal to give in and it draws on the deep strength which is there in all of us, if we dig deep enough to find it.

It is the will power that says 'I will keep going, this will get better'. Where does courage sit in our psyche and how can we access it? It sits deep within us, it is part of our survival kit and we can access it through our memories. There will be times in the past when we faced difficulties and we didn't give up. And while the journey might have been difficult and the outcome not necessarily what we wanted, in knowing that we didn't give up, we were strengthened in the process. It is drawing on previous times, when things are currently tough, that can provide the source of strength in current difficulties.

Settings that are courageous don't dodge the difficult issues. They know not to sweep things under the carpet, tempting as that might be. Courage is tough, it's not a soft option, because essentially it means not running away or taking the easy way out. When difficult decisions have to be made, for example, leaders having to restructure and possibly having to make people redundant, extra reserves of courage are needed. No one likes to be in the position of making others redundant. But the courage comes from taking a long view of the financial picture and taking the tough decisions. These are not taken lightly, but are approached with humility. And in seeing through the tough decision, they ensure that the individuals being made redundant are clear about the reasons why. That this is not personal, even though it might feel like that to those involved, and that every effort is made to ease their journey from the setting, recognising the value of the contributions they have made and ensuring that references reflect the quality of their work.

Then it takes courage for leaders in this scenario to rebuild the team. Not easy. Where it is done well, leaders give an overview of the reasons, emphasise the difficulty of the situation and acknowledge people's possible sadness and insecurity. This is tough and it has to be lived through day by day. There are no quick fixes.

It takes courage to stand up when things are wrong. When someone is being picked on or bullied or misunderstood. Those who are prepared to do this risk being in the firing line themselves. So courage sometimes comes at personal cost as well. Courage comes from knowing what the right thing is and being prepared to take a stand. The soft option is tempting. But it comes at a price of having to live with oneself afterwards. When just one person stands up to injustice and unfairness, they are encouraging others to do the same. Just through their actions.

Then there is the personal courage of people working, ploughing on, even in spite of physical and mental disability which might or might not be visible. Virtually everyone has a handicap of some sort. Whether it is a stammer, deafness, shyness, lack of confidence, we are all hampered in one way or another. Personal courage overcomes this, pushes through, and with it comes not only personal satisfaction, but respect from others. There are many who detest the idea of sharing their ideas in a large group. But they work to overcome their fear, because they know they have something important to share, and it is this that trumps their fear. And once they have done it, they often report a great sense of achievement. And the courage shown on that occasion can be drawn on for the next difficult task.

There are classrooms which talk about courage. Which encourage courage. These are where children are praised for the effort they have made, are shown just how far they have come and encouraged to talk about what it was like to learn something new and to make a good fist of it. Resilience is highly promoted in schools, but less is talked about the courage that it takes to work through misunderstandings, to do difficult, hard stuff when the temptation is to give up. It takes courage to tackle something we are unsure about, where we are worried we might fail and look stupid. It takes courage to pick ourselves up when we fall, when things are likely to go wrong. Any time a child picks up a new book or tackles a new maths challenge there is likely to be an element of fear. However, in classrooms where courage is talked about, they are able to see that part of themselves which gives them the strength and the energy to do the difficult.

And the final element in courage is keeping cheerful. Courage stops us from wallowing in thoughts about how difficult the potential barriers are. Instead, without diminishing them, they draw hope from the fact that they have overcome difficulties in the past. And when one person does it others see that it is possible to do the same.

31 Discretionary effort

'Continuous effort - not strength or intelligence - is the key to unlocking our potential.'
Winston Churchill

What is discretionary effort and how does it link to being hopeful rather than helpless? A job description or contract defines the role and scope of what we are expected to do. Much management theory and debate has taken place about what discretionary effort is and how it might have an impact on an organisation's success, and if so how this could be measured. It is possible that there is another way to look at this - the job can be done as a bare minimum or, I can bring my whole person, my whole self to the work I am doing. This is not about necessarily working more hours, or working harder, but it is more about seeing whether it is possible for my contribution to be consciously unique. However, I am only likely to bring this additional dimension to my work if I believe in it, if I believe that what I do is making a difference and I am hopeful that my efforts will make a difference. If I am feeling helpless, my horizons are likely to narrow, my focus is likely to be on getting by, getting through the day and less about contributing to a bigger picture.

This is likely to be at the heart of discretionary effort - the willingness to bring additional focus, care and imagination to my work. It is likely that imagination is the key to discretionary effort. I don't just see my job as the job in hand, but rather as something bigger. But I can only do this if I feel hopeful.

If organisations including schools want to open up and celebrate the notion of discretionary effort, they need to be painting a big picture of what the enterprise is about. Enterprises are more likely to help us feel hopeful, rather than helpless. I am more likely to engage and focus at a deeper level if I know what the big picture and the end goal are. Two examples: a medieval stonecutter at the early stages of building a cathedral while trimming the shapes to slot in to the wall. When asked what he was doing replied 'I am building an edifice to the glory of God.' He would never see the finished building, but his response says everything about the care and attention he was applying to the task in hand.

A later example: John Kennedy, when visiting Cape Canaveral and touring the NASA's Space Centre, asked one of the cleaners what his job involved. 'I am cleaning the floors and keeping the space immaculate, as part of my role in taking men to the moon.' It is possible to argue that both the stone cutter and the cleaner were doing the following as part of feeling hopeful about their role in the grand scheme of things: they were likely to be careful and precise, they were likely to self-regulate and to quality assure their own work, noticing whether they had missed anything, and they were likely to take a deeper pleasure in their work, than if they were not applying discretionary effort.

It is important that this kind of additional care and practice is not expected as a matter of course: that is why it is discretionary. Nor should it be pursued at an organisational level simply as a means of ratcheting up productivity and profitability. It is a much subtler way of working and of doing business and it cant be forced or expected. Instead, the conditions need to be created whereby the discretionary effort emerges because everyone, whatever their role feels hopeful about the work and the impact it has.

And when this idea is translated into schools, something very interesting happens. The adults believe in and act according to collective responsibility - they do not, for instance, walk past something that needs sorting; they back their colleagues up; they ask how they are; they praise one another for good work; they bring their ideas and suggestions and are happy to share these, without fear that they will be dismissed. And that is because the way of doing business in these organisations is hopeful, rather than helpless. It means that the site staff anticipate what might be needed, because they have been made to feel that their contribution is vital in the smooth running of the school. It means that reception staff understand that they are literally the first port of call for visitors, and that their welcome counts. It means that all teaching staff recognise their responsibility for the intellectual growth and nurture of all children in the school, not just the ones they teach. So they offer praise and encouragement, recognise good work well done and frame all this in terms of a hopeful future.

Most children want to help. They want to make a contribution. And wise schools tap into this natural desire the offer discretionary effort. It might not be called this, but they realise that children want to be creators as much as consumers. In these schools, children are asked what contribution they might make. And that is every child, not just those who are confident and outgoing. These schools understand that every child needs the space and opportunity to show what they can do and how they can enhance the learning for all. In these schools, children take on or support many of the roles done by adults - supervising lunches, taking registers, organising trips and visits outside of school. Not because the school sees this as cheap labour, but because they understand that children need opportunities for discretionary effort to emerge.

32 On labelling children

'It's very easy not to see the intelligence which is there'
Christopher Bryan

This is a sensitive topic. In every classroom there are children with different levels of prior attainment and with differing capacities to engage with the work. However, the labelling of children through setting might be putting limits on their learning.

What happens in many classrooms is that pupils are placed in groups which determine the level of work which they are expected to do. However these tables are labelled and however carefully the adults believe they have disguised the fact that they are given work of different challenge, children are remarkably astute at knowing what these mean. Whether they are on a table called leopards or lizards, they know what these signify. Whether they are number ones or number fours they know that this involves different levels of challenge and expectation. The problem comes when the labels remain stuck. Children self-identify with the level of work which is expected of them. This is not helpful either for the high prior attainers or the low prior attainers. The high attainers see themselves a privileged, as being worthy of greater challenge and as more able than others. All of which might be the case. But if their work drops and they are allocated a different label to differentiate their work they are likely to see themselves as failures. Similarly for the other labelled groups. Children who have the bottom labels, and they do know they are labelled bottom, feel that they cannot tackle more demanding work. They are often supported by an adult which is often appropriate. But what sometimes happens is that they become dependent on the adult to help them, even when they don't need it.

Alison Peacock in 'Assessment for Learning without Limits'[28] provides an insight into children's views on setting: 'The 'more able' loved it; they enjoyed being the 'bright' ones and having 'special' challenges set by the teacher. They also saw working with the teacher as a negative. The middle group were annoyed that they didn't get the same work and challenges as the other group; they wanted to try harder work but they have worked out they would never be moved up as there were only six seats on the top table. The 'less able' were affected the most. They felt 'dumb', useless, they thought they would never be allowed challenges as they usually work with the teaching assistant (some by year 5 were completely dependent on the teaching assistant to help them). This 'less able' group like the sound of some of the challenges the top group had, but knew they would never get the chance.'

For many of the 'lower' groups, they are offered closed responses - matching parts of sentences, filling in gaps, completing easy worksheets, none of which really stretches them or expects them to do much. Others, by contrast are given more to do and more is expected of them. While they might have a few closed exercises in order to practice or consolidate their knowledge, they are also expected to do new things with this - constructing their own sentences, coming up with other alternative adjectives in a piece of writing, suggesting alternatives to maths problems. These children are being given more opportunities both to struggle and to gain new knowledge. The others, by contrast, have insufficient expected of them and as a result, don't make the same gains as their peers. This extends the gap in their knowledge and attainment. The paradox is that by attempting to give them easier work, such exercises can often close down their capacity and opportunity to do more.

Teachers somehow have to make sense of this in order to get all children working to their highest capacity and potential. Schools which have recognised that grouping children by ability could be a problem in promoting self-limiting beliefs at all levels of ability have done away with the naming of tables or groups. Instead, they

28. www.amazon.co.uk/gp/product/0335261361/ref=pd_bxgy_14_img_3?ie=UTF8&psc=1&refRID=D646J1T742SM5F3Z0F0W

promote teaching to the top, rather than putting a lid on what children might produce by preparing materials which only allow them to go so far. The current trend in the teaching of mathematics in primary schools is that the whole class is taught together on the key ideas and those who need additional support are given this through guidance and discussion by an adult. Those who are early graspers are kept on the same material but are expected to work on aspects of greater complexity and depth.

The principle is that all children are exposed to the material at the same time. Now there will always be exceptions to this: those whose cognitive ability needs one-to-one support, often through pre-learning sessions so that they are able to access the material and others whose grasp is so secure early on that they need additional work which makes them really think. But for the majority of children in most classes the expectation is that by teaching to the top and providing additional support for those who need it and challenge for those who are capable of greater complexity. As a result all are exposed to a rich and demanding curriculum.

The shift in what pupils can do well in one lesson is likely to be different in another. So while a group of pupils might have grasped one aspect very quickly, they might be slower on another. This means that there needs to be fluidity and flexibility about what they do and what is expected of them. This movement in terms of expertise is natural. Not every child is going to struggle every time and not every child is going to race ahead. This is how learning works.

A compelling example for why it is so important not to underestimate what children can do. Jonathan Bryan, born with cerebral palsy after his mother was involved in a car accident started a campaign to ensure all children with 'locked-in' syndrome are taught to read and write[29]. It took seven years before he was able to communicate and now spends part of each day in the local primary school where he excels at maths. He also writes blogs and poems of great subtlety and wit and are read by thousands visiting his blog, 'Eye can talk: a silent soul emerging'[30].

---

29. www.dailymail.co.uk/news/article-3671847/The-lionhearted-Locked-Boy-Lad-trapped-silence-seven-years-miraculously-finding-way-signal-say-truly-astonish-you.html
30. www.eyecantalk.net/media/

So, a call to all to think about how we 'label' children and what might be hidden when we do so.

33 The expert novice conundrum

'An expert is a man who has made all the mistakes which can be made.'

Niels Bohr

We'd all love to be an expert. But the fact is that every expert started out as a novice. And the paradox is that the more expert someone is in their field the more they realise how much they don't know. The tease of expertise is that there is always more to do, to get to grips with, to understand. But when we are starting out on something there are numerous things that potentially get in the way of every feeling hopeful of becoming an expert: scant knowledge, no larger canvas on which to place new knowledge, patchy skills, poor strategies, many mistakes. All of which conspire to make us feel that we will never 'get' it.

So what happens on the journey from novice to expert? What differentiates those who get to a level of expertise from those who continue to flounder at the margins? There are possibly several things at play here: one is purpose, the notion that we are travelling in a direction which is worthwhile both for our learning and for the contribution we might make; another is the ability to have some insight into the struggles which others have had in gaining expertise; and another is a desire to get there.

To take these in turn. First, purpose. It helps if we know why we are doing something and what a final product or skill might look like. We are not inclined or encouraged to begin or keep going if we can't see the point of it. So it is important when we are starting out that we have a picture of what competence might look like.

Wise teachers understand this. They talk to pupils about how what they are learning is both important for its own sake and also for the wide horizons it might lead to. So a teacher explaining the importance of letters and sounds will also let children know that this is the key to reading all sorts of wonderful stuff, on their own. In an art lesson, pupils will be shown examples of artists' work which delight and confound. And they will be told that these artists were once like themselves, just starting out. And in English lessons, the power and beauty of poetry and stories will be shared and again the message is that this is possible for many of us, with hard work and application. No one was born being able to write, or draw or do maths. Even Nobel Prize winners and best-selling authors started at the bottom.

Secondly, when we understand the struggles which others have had in their journey to expertise and excellence, we are more likely to persevere. Too often examples of outstanding work are portrayed as though they emerged, fully formed from the expert's mind. Very rarely are drafts and mistakes shown. Very rarely are the personal struggles shared. And this is a pity because the final products with their polish and wit will often appear to be beyond the capability of a novice. To counter this, some schools make a point of exploring the life stories of famous authors, mathematicians and scientists. In part because this is interesting work and in part to show that these people did not produce work that was fully formed at the start. They often had to flee as refugees, they often had to supplement their living by doing other jobs, they were often criticised and jeered at for their attempts. In gaining some insight into their struggles we are able to put our own efforts and our failures into context. It provides a canvas to be hopeful and it creates the conditions for us to persevere.

And finally, there has to be a desire to get there. Learning something new and gaining expertise is not something which can be forced on us. It is the case, that up to a certain point extrinsic factors come in to play - our pupils might want to do something to get a good grade, to do well in examinations, to gain the approval of others

- there is nothing wrong with these per se, but it is probable that they only take us so far. Real expertise comes at a cost. If the only rewards are extrinsic then once these external factors have gone, the resolve and the motivation are in danger of being reduced. However, the personal desire to achieve is of a completely different order. Here, it is the internal satisfaction gained from seeing improvement, of working towards a goal. When this is secure, it means that we are able to take setbacks and discouragement in our stride. The pleasures and the pain are private. That is not to say that these can't be shared with others, but they are not reliant on the approval or otherwise of other people.

So what constitutes this journey from novice to expert? It is one of trial and error, where mistakes are seen as opportunities for new learning. It is one where we need an expert to show us the bigger picture, to talk about their struggles to make it, to help us to see the funny side of things going wrong and to help us see where we might take it. These experts need to give us the tools to be as efficient as possible but they will not underplay the level of effort and commitment required. They will however, celebrate the small milestones on the way. And they will encourage us to say, at regular intervals, look how far I've come! Not in a boastful way but in the sense of self-encouragement - a short while ago I could only do this and now I can do that. This is powerful indeed and shifts the emphasis from what can't be done to what is now being done, to what it is possible to be done. From hopeless to hopeful.

34 The feeling of dread

'As much as we thirst for approval we dread condemnation.'
Hans Selye

There is an obligation on all of us to treat people kindly. We have all been misjudged or picked up on for something which was unfair, so it is likely that most of know what this feels like. How then is it possible to do this to someone else? Most people's self-esteem is not rock solid. Teaching is tough and most people in the business are trying to do a good job. So why is that some leaders feel entitled to belittle others and to put them down? When this happens, it doesn't take long for a spiral of hopelessness to occur. And this can have a trickle-down effect which can lead to widespread demoralisation.

This feeling can result when people are told that what they are doing isn't good enough, that their lesson is 'inadequate', or they are perceived not to be fulfilling their role or responsibilities. It makes the recipient of such comments feel wretched and inadequate as professionals and as people. And the more so when the comments made are unfair. If the person making them has not seen whole picture, not appraised themselves of a situation, or has misinterpreted guidance and then made the wrong judgements, the feeling of inadequacy and injustice is felt even more keenly.

Let's take an example of lesson observation feedback and how it can go wrong. A lesson observer concluded after 20 minutes observation that pupils had made insufficient progress. (As an inspector, progress in twenty minutes is, in my view a ridiculous expectation.) It is highly unlikely that the observer, or in fact the vast majority of teachers, would be able to demonstrate progress in twenty minutes. This is not how learning works.

There are two things wrong with this particular feedback - the first is that the leader observing a section of a lesson was misinterpreting an understanding of progress from an inspection point of view. Progress has always been framed in terms of 'over time' which is over a key stage. And it is possible to have some evidence of this from a school's data about pupils' scores at key stage 2 and at GCSE. This is over several years, not twenty minutes.

The second thing that is wrong with it was that the observer was making a judgement on the overall quality of someone's professional work on the basis of a short observation. Pupils' progress is judged from a range of sources - their end of key stage tests, internal tests, their written work, their conversations and other 'products' which show what they have learnt. It should be obvious that when following inspection guidance about lesson observations, the observer is able to interpret correctly. So, from a false premise, the observer in this example was causing considerable harm.

If a teacher raises concerns about a judgement, with evidence to back their case, such concerns must not be dismissed.

There need to be channels by which a teacher who has been unfairly treated on the basis of misjudgement can be heard. Otherwise, where is the humanity? How are people meant to carry on if they are made to feel that their work is worthless?

The focus for anyone going into someone else's lesson should be what pupils are doing and how it relates to learning. Nothing else. It should always be supportive, never threatening, demeaning or belittling.

There are times when we get things wrong. We can be abrupt, say things without thinking or not realising the impact that our words are having.

So two things need to happen. The first is that we need to reflect continuously on how we deal with others, particularly if we hold leadership positions. We need to ensure that we have made thorough preparation for such things as lesson observations or other encounters with our colleagues which require giving feedback or making judgements. And if we realise that we have been harsh, be humble and big-hearted enough go back and check that they are all right. It is as simple as that.

The second is that if someone tells us that we have been unfair, that we are open enough to listen, reflect *and* apologise. If that had happened in the lesson observation example, there would not have been a shattering of confidence or feelings of inadequacy.

We have a real duty to be kind to one another.

35 Something to do

'Three grand essentials to happiness in this life are something to do, something to love, and something to hope for.'
Joseph Addison

The first, something to do. For those of us lucky enough to have a job, let's pause for a moment to think about what that means in connection to feeling hopeful, not helpless. No job is perfect, but the fact we have one is better than not having one. A bit of a statement of the obvious, but a part of the hopeful agenda is about not taking things for granted. The key is to look at the job fairly and squarely, warts and all. Quite often the rotten bits take up more of our headspace than the better bits. So it is an idea to catch ourselves when we are focusing again on what is making us frustrated, angry or out of the loop. It is not about dismissing these, but instead holding them in balance with the better aspects. And there is always something which is great about what we do, even if it is quite small. This is not about minimising the negative, but remembering to notice the good as well.

And 'something to do' is about more than formal work. It is the contribution we make to our families, friends and wider society. Being involved with something bigger than ourselves both gives us something to work on and to think about, beyond our own petty worries. The team spirit which emerges from taking part in sports, whether physically or as an observer, the involvement in an allotment, the contribution to a charity, are all reasons for helping us to recognise the merits of having something to do. It stops us from being on auto-pilot and helps us to refocus on the better things in life. And this in turn makes a contribution to feeling hopeful, not helpless.

The second, something to love. There is some fairly strong evidence on the impact of owning a pet.[31] Why is this? It is possible that owning a pet takes the focus off ourselves, makes us concerned with the welfare and well-being of another being. And there is deep contentment and satisfaction in that. And the same goes whether one owns a pet, or not. Anyone who celebrates wildlife, whether they own a pet themselves or not, is testament to the fact that focusing on another living thing, brings its own joy and satisfaction. It takes us to the world beyond ourselves, to the wider connections of other lives.

And the same applies to children, whether they are our own, or those we teach. The professional 'loving' is fundamentally different, obviously from the love of a parent for a child. Both involve the tough love and care. But the professional love is concerned more with the cognitive development day by day for the child. And the warmth and good humour generated by what the Greeks called *agapé* has a depth which adds considerably to the satisfaction and enjoyment of professional life.

Something to hope for: this is fundamental. A life without hope is one of darkness and sadness. And it is often linked to depression, when nothing seems worth it, when the skies are dark, literally and metaphorically and where no ray of sunshine seems visible on the horizon. A dark place to be. And there are likely to be times, in everyone's life, when this is the case. So it is important to inoculate ourselves against the potentially dark times by making an effort to be hopeful. There are times when this is easier than at others, but like any skill, it gets better with practice. There must always be hope for a better world, where people are treated with respect, and while the news is often full of stories of the opposite, our role is to try and act counter to this, in every interaction we have, in every day life. It chimes with the Gandhi's famous principle 'You must be the change you want to see in the world' where the thinking is that we cannot change everything, but we can start with ourselves. For example, Martha Payne, a pupil in Scotland, blogged about her school lunches and rated them for healthiness and taste. After it

---

31. thepsychologist.bps.org.uk/volume-24/edition-3/value-pets-human-health

gained considerable publicity she used this springboard to raise money for a campaign to support the charity 'Mary's lunches' for school children in Malawi.

It is the taking of action which provides hope. This is what marks it out from wishful thinking. And it is important to distinguish between realistic and unrealistic hope. Unrealistic hope focuses on wishing for things which are not only unlikely to occur, but which take no effort on our part. These might include, winning the lottery (well, there is an outside chance of that), all our luck changing and being whisked off to a fairy tale existence. Realistic hope on the other hand, involves our taking both some responsibility and some action on our part. So, when we talk about hoping for a better atmosphere at work, what are we going to do to make that more likely to happen? Or, we hope that our difficult groups are going to behave better and concentrate in class - well exactly who is going to help us with that, if needed and how are we going to make these 'hopes' explicit to the awkward crew?

And the hope we have both for ourselves and for those who are dear to us. What will we do to take the first steps to make these a reality? Often it starts with giving first, without expectation of anything in return.

36 Hope in the community

'Every successful individual knows that his or her achievement depends on a community of persons working together'
Paul Ryan

The principles of making a contribution and expecting pupils to make a contribution is alive and well in many schools. What happened in the Room 13 project was that it emerged from a particular set of circumstances, through pupils' requesting to take something further and through school leaders giving them enough room to crack on and do it on their own terms. Other schools too have taken the idea, not necessarily inspired by Room 13 but certainly by its principles. These schools say, 'we have some resources here, identified in our school community, our local area, our parents, so where might this go?'

There are schools which are thinking carefully both about their place in the community and the resources which a local community can offer in return.

At a basic level, many schools open up their sports and meeting facilities to the wider community - this both produces income and widens access so that the school is seen as a natural and welcoming place for community activities.

Many seek opportunities to bring in the wider community as often as possible. One special school in Cheshire invites local schools to its exhibitions and drama productions. And it takes its pupils to other schools to do the same. The relationships, learning and friendship which emerge from this mean that not only are both communities more connected but shared activities create the conditions for more hope for all.

When schools are thinking about how to involve parents, some are inviting them to become involved in running their school allotment. Penair School in Truro[32] involves families with children who are under 5 growing fruit and vegetables together. In doing this, these schools are creating honest activities which draw parents in. They in turn are able to make a contribution and the children delight in the results.

Similarly, many schools are providing opportunities to make links with the local community, for example visiting local care homes. While many visit to share productions, others are encouraging older pupils to make regular contact with older people in their community. Pupils from Azhar Academy[33] found that this was not a one-sided benefit. While visits are welcomed by those in care homes, there were great benefits for pupils as well who found it an effective way of learning about the history of life in east London. In creating 'Lifebooks' for residents – a collection of stories, quotes and photographs about their lives, they both reflected back the highlights of the lives of older people and gained an insight into both the wisdom and loneliness of some of the older people. The takeaway point from this example is that such activities are not always easy or comfortable. But they are worthwhile in that deeper connections, and as a result, the potential for hope is increased.

Mayflower Academy engages with the wider community to break down boundaries, broaden horizons and provide high quality learning experiences, both in and out of school, that help children develop a love of learning new things and a strong sense of citizenship. What is interesting about the work at Mayflower, is that it takes 'wider community' in its broadest meaning. Under the leadership of the headteacher Dave Sammels, the school has trained a number of local people in catering. Some of these have gone on to full-time employment. What is also interesting is that these opportunities came about through opening up the school restaurant for family meals in the evening. There are plans to extend these over the weekends as well.

---

32. schoolgardening.rhs.org.uk/school-stories/Happy-Days-Nursery-Penair

33. www.newhamrecorder.co.uk/news/girls_from_islamic_school_visit_the_elderly_in_east_ham_care_home_1_3491435

A school, both at the heart of its community and providing hope for those looking for new opportunities.

The Swiss Cottage School works with children with multiple and profound complex needs. Its work on curriculum and assessment is recognised internationally. What is so special about their work? Well one aspect is, that it believes that much of the children's work should have an authentic audience and where possible involve the wider community. This is not about every piece of work - there are basic things to be learnt and practised - spellings and times tables, for example. These are the essential building blocks for bigger work and they are not compromised. However, there are larger pieces of work where the final product is expected to be shown to a wider audience. In one example, they show how two pupils engage with a curriculum. In this case, the end goal is to perform a piece of music in front of a live audience. For one pupil, they are shown the nuts and bolts e.g. the number of strings on a guitar and the 'learning' is ticked off on a spreadsheet. For another pupil, the teacher encourages the child to play with a tambourine, then working up to playing the guitar. The journey is messier, the learning sometimes goes backwards, but the final product is a performance in front of parents and friends. Unlike the first child who only has a series of ticks to his name. What the school is showing in this example is that the prospect of creating something to perform in front of others has the power and the potential for a pupil to be hopeful about what they can achieve.

37 Showing up

'Show up, speak up, look up, start every meeting with why we do this, vision and values; team up (everything goes better with partners); never give up, everything can look like a failure in the middle; lift others up

Rosabeth Moss Kanter

'Everything can look like a failure in the middle' according to Rosabeth Moss Kanter, Professor of Business at the Harvard Business School. And who's not been there at some point? We start off a new venture full of ideas and hope and there nearly always comes a time when the slog sets in, when we don't get the response we want, it is all taking longer and proving harder than we expected. Moss Kanter has worked with hundreds of organisations and her advice is particularly pertinent to the theme of hopeful not helpless.

First, showing up. There is no point in running away, in absenting ourselves from the work in hand. Credit and rewards over time, go to those who stick with the work, through the tough as well as the easy times. Showing up is a discipline. By refusing to give up and resisting the urge to be either physically or mentally absent creates resilience and power in the long term. It also sets an example to others. And when our students turn up, day in day out, often in spite of challenging circumstances at home, they are more likely to reap the rewards over time. So, if showing up is important in developing the perseverance to keep going, this is worth talking about. Professionals on the one hand are paid to show up, but it can be tempting to show up physically, but not make the real effort to engage. In other words to be mentally and emotionally absent. Paying attention is the way to over come this. Giving respect to ourselves and others for sticking things through over the long haul, will make the final rewards sweeter. It is also important for building our own value and respect for ourselves. 'I am the sort of person who shows up, even when it is difficult.'

And once we've turned up, it is important to speak up. Everyone has a contribution to make. And however lacking in confidence we might feel, it is important that we put our point of view, make a contribution and respond to those of others. People often say that they don't have anything worthwhile to say. But how will they ever really know if they don't offer something? One way of looking at this is to remind ourselves that if we don't say or contribute anything we are denying others the particular insights which we have. As long as the principles of 'high challenge, low threat' are respected, where no one is made to feel a Muppet for expressing a point of view, this should be fine. And if the culture isn't right, then who is going to say something about it, if not you? No matter where we are in an organisation, the fact that we are there at all, gives us the right to contribute.

Then to 'look up'. This is great advice. There is always something bigger to move towards. There is always a worthwhile goal. And if that isn't the case, then should you be working on it? Assuming that it is worthwhile, the looking up helps us to see the big picture we are working towards. The looking up allows us to see beyond our own petty concerns and worries to something which is bigger than us and which is making a contribution to our setting and also to wider society. The focus of the looking up also provides us with inspiration - this is where we are, but this is where we are heading. And that has tremendous power to help us feel hopeful, not helpless.

We should also be starting every meeting with why we are doing this - this helps us to clarify the bigger picture we are working on. It helps us to keep, in the words of Stephen Covey the 'main thing the main thing'. And it cuts through the current hot topics, news and gossip to get us to focus on the heart of the matter.

Teaming up with others can make us more productive, help us to see the bigger picture and can contribute to feeling hopeful not helpless. Beyond the cliché of a problem shared being a problem halved, the balance of solo and participative work stops us feeling alone and alienated when things get tough. And tough is a given in any worthwhile endeavour. The conditions for this working well though, mean that those we team up with need to be in the same 'space' as the bigger picture - where there is no room for egos, only for a collective contribution which draws on everyone's talents to achieve a goal. This is not to deny the importance of solo and solitary work, because this is needed as well. But it is in the joint collaboration at strategic points which lifts us from the mundane to the extraordinary.

'Never give up' because it's in the hardest and darkest of times that the insights and the new moves are made. When we make a commitment to never give up, we are aligning ourselves with the great achievers, people who get stuff done. These are often beyond the headlines - the mother who never gives up on her child with additional needs, the teacher who refuses to accept that any child in her class cannot read, the leader who knows that improvement is possible. And it is in the commitment to never giving up that we create our own rock-solid self-esteem. Something is important and I am going to stick with it. There is tremendous power in that. And particularly important when we are going through what feels like 'failure' in the middle of a project.

And finally, lift others up. Why? Because it is the greatest way to bolster our own self-esteem, to move from hopeless to helpless. It is one of the greatest things we can offer to another human being. Whatever their age, whatever their position.

38 The culture of giving

'Every time we interact with another person at work, we have a choice to make: do we try to claim as much value as we can, or contribute value without worrying about what we receive in return?'

Adam Grant

How does giving relate to being hopeful? It might sound counter-intuitive to argue that by giving something away, whether it is money, things or our time that it makes us more hopeful. It looks as though the act of giving benefits not just the receiver but the giver too. Why might this be? Well, most of us experience deep satisfaction when we do something that makes something or someone else better. It speaks to our capacity for goodness, for capability and for potential. And it is this which results in our being hopeful, not helpless. It shines a light on the capacity we have to make a difference both to ourselves and to others - if we can support others then we must have something in us which is valued and of use to others.

There is potential for greater energy and efficiency being released in schools which understand this. It works on two strands - the first is that people understand the power of giving and the impact it has on their own well being, on the healthy atmosphere in their setting and the general vibes of goodwill. However if they recognise that this is true for them, then they work on the second strand, which is this: if giving is a good thing, then all should be provided with opportunities to make a contribution. This cannot be forced. But it can be talked about.

In some schools which recognise this, leaders not only give

themselves e.g. their time, their willingness to listen, but also spot opportunities for younger members of the staff to give, if they so choose. So, when a new piece of work or project is being considered, they ask who might want to contribute to this, take the lead on this? Not because they have to, but because they choose to. For example, when new ideas to support the promotion of spiritual, moral, social and cultural development are available, these are offered as a way of extending thinking and expertise. It provides an opportunity for someone who feels they would like to make a contribution to explore these areas and devise creative ways of incorporating them more deeply in the curriculum. This makes it light touch - a matter of reading up on the ideas, and talking through what children might do. It won't need a massive report or a big spreadsheet - but it will need an audience, usually a slot at a staff meeting to hear what the volunteer has found. It may also provide opportunities for a small classroom-based action research project in which the volunteer can involve others who are interested in being involved.

Similarly with the development of numeracy across the curriculum - the maths lead might open it up for discussion about who would like to do some thinking about this. Not as an added burden but as an opportunity to make a contribution. This removes the obligation and places it instead in the space of voluntary contribution. This is possible when the fundamentals are in place - the overall curriculum plans. This is about taking the refinement to the next level and inviting people to make a contribution.

The same applies in the classroom. Children want to make a contribution and wise teachers harness this. Why would any child not clear away after themselves? Why would they not be taught how to console someone who is sad? Why would they not be asked what they would like to 'give' - not necessarily in material things but rather their ideas, their research, their stories and their anecdotes.

Some secondary schools have worked out that their students need more opportunities to make a contribution - not just for the satisfaction of doing good work, but also to give them opportunities to lead and take responsibility. And so what some of these are doing is identifying those jobs or projects which could usefully be done by students: rather than asking an adult in the school to arrange a visit to a museum, art gallery or place of worship, they are bringing small groups of students together and asking them to do the research: the location of the venue, admission charges, additional guides, travel costs, health and safety and drafting letters to parents and carers.

What this is doing is creating the space for young people to 'give' - of their time, their organisation, their imagination. And none of their work and research goes beyond the school, until it has been checked by a member of staff, who acts in a sense as a managing director. The project needs to be signed off by them. But in the process, what has happened? The adults have saved valuable time. The students have been given the chance to plan something from scratch, to research and to prioritise and to produce a plan which has to be signed off. And because they have volunteered for this, they have an opportunity to give on their own terms.

And there is research to support this. Researchers at the University of Notre Dame in Indiana have shown that generosity has been shown to boost immunity, improve mental health, increase physical strength, and release hormones that enhance happiness.

Giving and simple acts of kindness benefit not only others, but also the giver. But giving isn't just beneficial to health - it can also play a key role in success. Adam Grant, Wharton Professor of Management, has compared the outcomes between 'givers' versus 'takers'. He found that the givers ultimately rise to the top because of their selfless approach to networking and collaboration. In giving someone something - whether it's time, resources, energy - you create a dynamic where the recipient appreciates and feels compelled to return the favour, often going above and beyond the original gift. It's a win-win scenario.

The best part about giving back is that there are no losers, only winners. No matter how you choose to incorporate generosity into your life, you're actively helping both others and yourself. However, this doesn't mean completely we need to take ourselves and our priorities and well-being out of the picture; it is possible do both at once. What is important is to give in a genuine, sincere way to something we actually care about. As Grant says, 'If you only do it to succeed, it probably won't work'.

So, wise schools are thinking hard about opportunities for staff and pupils to give as well as receive. It has the capacity to release tremendous stuff.

Section 5
Wider examples of hope

39 Be a lamp

Be a lamp, a lifeboat, a ladder. Help someone's soul heal.
Walk out of your house like a shepherd.
Rumi

How does being a lamp help us to feel hopeful rather than helpless? Surely we should be expecting something or someone to be the lamp for us? Well, there is something interesting at play here. When we offer our lamp or light to others, in terms of encouragement, support or giving them hope, we are also building our own light. The effect turns into a virtuous circle, where the good we extend to others comes back to us. According to Marianne Williamson[34], 'as we let our own light shine, we unconsciously give other people permission to do the same.' And the thing is that the light does not have to be big, bright and showy. It can provide quiet comfort on the one hand, through a gesture or a word, it can spread out and be more expansive....

And the light can also be seen as showing the way. Where we go first, show courage in difficult circumstances we are giving others hope in the process. There is always someone watching us, not in an Orwellian, undercover way, but in the simple terms of the fact that our actions are noticed, either consciously or subliminally by others. And we have the choice either to be a light or to snuff it out with negativity. And when this happens we snuff out our own as well.

The lifeboat in Rumi's quote is not necessarily a literal lifeboat, but rather a metaphor for extending a hand, a listening ear to others

---

34. www.goodreads.com/quotes/928-our-deepest-fear-is-not-that-we-are-inadequate-our

who might need it. And this can be done at little cost to ourselves. Often the gesture of a smile or an encouraging word, sincerely meant is like lifting a sparrow on the ground, back into flight. The point about the lifeboat is to be alert, without being a martyr to the needs of others. Our greatest need is for connection with others, and not just material help. Examples of this - in one school where a very talented newly qualified teacher was struggling with the paperwork to complete his first year, all the staff, led by the head stayed behind one day after school, to work with him on it. Without that lifeboat, he would have been unlikely to have completed his year and the profession would have lost a fine teacher. What he learned from that experience of being helped to complete his assignment, was organisation, cutting through to the things that really matter and making sure that he was better organised when another big piece of work came his way. And he also understood what it felt like to be supported by colleagues. And when his turn came, he was able to offer others similar practical support.

The ladder one is interesting. It could be seen as a prostrating oneself, putting their needs before our own, turning us into servile nobodies. Or it can be read in another way - that the strength of the ladder provides the steps to support others. Some of whom would not get off the ground without our support and some of whom might go on to do even bigger and better things than imagined either by us or them. The ladder needs a solid foundation on which to rest - this might be the community support around us; it might be our strength of belief and purpose, honed through our own struggles, strife and triumphs. And we can only aspire to be the ladder if we have the capacity to support not just ourselves but others.

So how might this work in a school setting? It could be used as a metaphor for discussions in meetings about values admission statements. Who are our ladders? Who do we provide ladders for? In what way might our children become ladders for others? And what does it say about our community if we think about our roles as ladders?

Helping to heal someone's soul might sound like evangelising. But Rumi was a Persian poet and theologian, and whether we are religious or not, we can take some insight from this. All of us as we go through life, are bruised and hurt. Our spirit gets dented, we lose heart and are tempted to give up. And I think it is in this sense that Rumi is best understood - that the sadness which is part of the human condition can be assuaged by healing. So what do we mean by healing? It is the making whole, patching up the injury and injustice as we go through life. The balm can be provided through gestures, words or deeds. The important thing is that they are offered with humility, no sense of showmanship, but rather in the spirit of a fellow traveller through life. The giving of this is, paradoxically, the fuel for our own aspirations for being hopeful as opposed to helpless.

And when the tables are turned, and we are on the receiving end of healing, we have to be careful not to brush it away. It is like a gift which is being offered, where the donor is giving away a part of themselves, making themselves vulnerable, in order to give solace to us. And it can come from anywhere - a friend, a colleague, a stranger and even a tiny child in our classroom who picks up that we are sad and asks whether we are ok. It is in the asking whether we are ok that the child is providing the balm to heal our soul. This is not a magic wand taking the pain away, but rather the sympathetic gesture of one human to another.

And what a great image of 'walking out of our house like a shepherd' - a good shepherd, who looks out for the flock, who takes pride in their thriving and who treats them like a good parent. That's it. How would it be if we all set out in the morning, determined to look out for one another?

40 No dry holes

'It's so easy to string together a bunch of platitudes and call them a mission statement. But what happens if you actually have a specific mission, a culture in mind, a manifesto for your actions?'

Seth Godin

BP finds oil in two out of three of its drilling explorations. That is three times higher than the industry standard. How do they do this? They came up with the slogan, 'no dry holes' because they realised that drilling in an ad hoc way, was wasteful in terms of time and resources. This had been sustainable in the days of 'Spindletop oil' in the early 1900s when huge oil fields were first discovered in Texas, but this is not sustainable when wells were costing up to 40 million dollars to get working. The earlier theory had been, if we are successful in one in ten then that is fine. But with rising costs, strategy needed to be sharper.

So the mantra became 'no dry holes'. What was the effect of this? It meant that geologists had to make a compelling case before ordering up a rig. Now the geologists at BP probably thought they were doing everything they could already, so what it needed was a shift in thinking. A commitment to doing fewer things in greater depth, literally. This is a tough discipline and it can feel counterintuitive particularly before the results are seen. The temptation is usually to do more of the same in the hope of different results.

How might 'no dry holes' translate elsewhere? What might a school look like which adopted this simplified strategy? What would the equivalent of 'no dry holes' look like in a school? Well, if we take the example of BP again, the first insight is to ask 'what is the big piece of work which needs to be done here?' What is the problem that needs to be addressed? In the oil industry it had been accepted that many attempts at digging wells were needed before reliable sources of oil were found. With rising costs, BP realised that it needed a vision which said, things could be different. So, what is the underlying 'big, hairy goal' in a school? In a primary school, it might be, every child a reader. In a secondary, it might be all students at 16 reaching a positive value-added score in their GCSEs.

In a school which had historically found that some parents were reluctant to come in and meet teachers, the big goal might be translated into 'everyone welcome'. Now, if everyone really is welcome, what does that mean? Are the receptionists welcoming towards everyone, even the awkward squad? If they are, this doesn't happen by accident. They in turn have been made to feel welcome by leaders of the school. They are appreciated for their work, often difficult, unsung work. And leaders do this by noticing, talking about it and thanking them for the great contribution they make to the school. Everyone appreciates being told they are doing a good job. So it means, that if they have been appreciated for what they have done in the past, they are likely to be open to conversations about how to make things even better.

This moves the agenda away from, how can I get away with the least possible, to how can I give my highest contribution? Because in this thought experiment, the big mantra has been 'everybody welcome'. It is a phrase which everyone can use, can understand and where it is very clear whether it has happened, or not. It also shifts the focus from helpless to hopeful.

When we have committed to a big mantra, over time, it permeates our behaviour and our attitude to everything. However, it has to be deeply and truly meant and embraced. It is no good paying lip service to it, because lip service stays on the lips. It doesn't change anything. In the same way that 'no dry holes' was a phrase to drive all thinking about finding oil, so 'everyone welcome' would need to drive all thinking and behaviour within a school. And this is not necessarily easy, because it is one thing to welcome those we like, or those who are like us. But what about those who are not like us and who we don't necessarily like?

That is where the depth comes from. If we are working to these principles, then it has to go deep and embrace the tough stuff as well. And that is when the transformation takes place. And then to the classroom. What does it look like here, if we decide that 'everyone is welcome'? It means that the teacher and adults working with children, are genuinely pleased to see the children. They talk about this and about how they are looking forward to working with them today. The talk about how all their contributions are welcome.

And they talk about what it means to be made to feel welcome. What it means to make someone else feel welcome. What the difference is between just saying the words and really meaning it. What happens when we are not made to feel welcome? What sort of work are we prepared to do when this is the case? How does that compare with feeling welcome? What is the difference?

These are big, demanding pieces of work. But what they also have about them is simplicity. They are something which everyone can understand. It is very easy to see whether they are being acted on or not, very easy to check whether it is real. And above all, they have the power to make all of us feel hopeful, not helpless.

41 Someone else's problem

"Nothing at Facebook is someone else's problem." When you see something that's broken, go fix it.'

The philosophy that gets adopted doesn't mean that you have to be constantly looking for problems outside of your realm, as it has over 500 programmers, but Kent Beck, a programmer, explains that it is very rare to hear someone say that an issue isn't their problem.

"If they do say that, they will get clear and immediate feedback that it is not how we do things. It will be very uncomfortable for them, as it is a fundamental thing that makes Facebook different."[35]

How does this notion of personal responsibility play into being hopeful not helpless? I think it has to do with agency. Now we are not talking here about wading in to every little thing, or taking over when something is already under control. But it is about offering a hand, if and when needed. This might sound like a statement of the obvious, but it's remarkable the difference it makes when it is properly embedded in a culture.

Then, instead of people walking by when there is poor behaviour, ignoring litter, or letting individuals struggle with a task or project on their own, there is a gentle layer of support which means that no individual is ever left out in the cold, to struggle with things on their own. And if this is the culture, then what applies to all, will apply to the individual self as well. There are some laws at work, that if I offer help to others, by and large it comes back to me.

But more than that, it helps to bring an organisation together. The team is bigger than any individual. It turns organisations, no matter what their size, into humane settings. So, what are some of

---

35. www.htxt.co.za/2015/08/26/nothing-at-facebook-is-someone-elses-problem-and-thats-why-it-works-so-well/

the consequences when we take the view that 'it's not someone else's problem'?

The first is, that it makes us all more efficient. This might sound counter-intuitive, but the reality is that if everyone is pitching in, things get done faster, and the ragged edges in the running of a setting disappear. This happens outside of work as well. When family and friends collaborate over the preparation and clearing up of a meal for example, it not only makes the whole thing go more smoothly and efficiently, there is often a kind of camaraderie which emerges. The sweet spirit of a joint endeavour. This happens in schools, where a group of colleagues will help a new arrival to the school set up their classroom, organise resources and clear away any debris from the previous term. It works when there are whole school activities such as fêtes, parents' evenings, when colleagues don't just sort themselves out, but look to see if they can make a wider contribution.

The second is that it makes us feel good. When we make a contribution, a wider effort beyond our own narrow world, it brings with it a deep satisfaction of making a difference. And it is this which contributes to feeling hopeful, not helpless. When we are part of a larger endeavour, when we can see the results of our input jointly with others, it brings great satisfaction of a job well done, with others. There is something to be gained from contributing to a piece of work, which is bigger than us and which involves other people.

The third is that it makes an organisation more cohesive. The involvement of all and the expectation that all will be involved means that people are encouraged to look beyond their narrow roles and responsibilities. When this happens, my contribution to my aspect of work is one element, but I also have an obligation to meet the needs of the whole group. This is not to sacrifice my individuality, nor to become a workaholic, but rather to incorporate it within the daily attitude of going about my business. Classrooms which get this right encourage all children to take responsibility for the atmosphere in the classroom: is it conducive to learning, is everyone pulling their weight, is everyone clearing up after themselves, is everyone making sure that all are welcome, is everyone brought in to offer their own individual gifts to the group?

The further aspect which is playing in to this, is everyone's need to be needed. There is no greater compliment to be paid to someone than 'Can you help me? I need your advice'. What that is doing is affirming mastery and expertise in a subject or skill, which is being asked for by another. In this transaction, the gift of one is passed to the other. And while the person who has done the giving might be seen to have lost something, in fact the opposite is usually true - their skill and expertise has been acknowledged by another and is sought after. This is likely to encourage them to develop their expertise even further. In settings which value and honour the worth of every individual, it becomes common practice to offer a contribution wherever and whenever this is needed.

However, this can only work in high functioning settings. There is a potential danger if this innate willingness to make a contribution is exploited by leaders. People know when they are being taken for granted. They know when they are expected to do something which others aren't prepared to do and they know when there is cynical exploitation. Which is why it is no coincidence that in the top performing, highly cohesive settings both in education and elsewhere, that leaders make a point of never asking anyone to do something which they have not either done themselves, or are still prepared to do and demonstrate it, by doing so regularly. Everyone getting their hands dirty is the way to secure this. And everyone means everyone.

42 On second chances

'We all need a second chance sometimes'
Joel Osteen

What we can learn from other sectors that might support practice in schools? If we want people to be hopeful, to get better and to have an impact, it is important that they are given opportunities to show what they can do. If we assume that most people want to do the right thing most of the time, then we can afford to take some risks. At Timpson, the shoe repairers and key cutters it has long been a policy to employ people who have been in prison. They have 270 staff, 10 per cent of the workforce, some of whom work in the shops during the day, return to jail at night under the Prison Service's Release on Temporary Licence scheme. Why would any company take a risk with people who are ex-convicts?

For a start, they are careful about who they employ and in the early days of the project, discovered that things could go badly wrong. But through careful vetting what they have found is that by setting out minimum, but high expectations in terms of financial probity and courtesy with customers, is that it does work. Generally, not always, because that is life. But if people know where they stand, what is expected of them and are given a chance, by and large they live up to it.

This is a carefully thought through philosophy, translated into business practice. It is not some well-intentioned philanthropic gesture; it is rooted in the world and the metrics of the bottom line, of profits, of shareholder and stakeholder accountability. So what is going on here and why does it work? It works because it is grounded in the real world; it works because it sees people as having potential. It sees the commercial merit in giving people a fresh start and a clean state. It also comes from a place which acknowledges that we are all human and that we have all made mistakes. It creates the circumstances where people are able to rise to their best selves without recrimination for what might have gone before.

This creates a culture where the whole organisation is more profitable by creating opportunities for people who have everything to gain from proving themselves. And it also expects them to make a contribution. This is something which has real power in schools - there is always a small minority who are disaffected, whose families are disaffected and who are regularly in trouble. Quite often the sanctions don't work. And that is possibly because they are not shown how they might be better and are not given opportunities to show that they can be better. And most importantly to make a contribution.

In some schools which have recognised this, they make a point of looking for opportunities for these pupils to make a contribution to school life. It shifts the onus from sanctions (which might still be necessary) but balances these with an expectation that they contribute. What happens when people are expected to make a contribution is that the focus on behaviour shifts from a deficit model, of what has gone wrong, to a plentiful model of what they might do better. And they can show that they can be better by making a contribution. Some schools have taken risks by asking these students to work on some aspect of school life - for example, leading a research group on how the school environment can be improved, on a limited budget, carrying out surveys such as parents' and carers' views of the school, pupils' views of the school, the local community's views of the school. What is happening here is that rather than an adult in the school doing all the administration and research, a group of students are asked to do this and to report back. Nothing leaves the school until it has been signed off by a teacher. But the points is, they have done the work, engaged with organisations beyond the school and have taken on a significant piece of work for which they are recognised. As one of our deepest needs is to be recognised and affirmed this has a double effect of getting some important work done and positioning these students as the 'experts' in researching and organising this. Schools which have experimented with this, have found that these students become more engaged, because they have a stake in the successful outcomes of the survey which will in turn impact on the school. They can point to something where they were trusted to get on and produce results. They can put this on their CV, but more importantly they have a sense of achievement from being trusted. As a result of this exercise they have become 'experts' in aspects of researching, planning and organising which can be then used in other contexts.

Is this likely to make them feel more hopeful rather than helpless? Those students spoken to have said how much they appreciated being given a chance to show what they can do, rather than always being told off for the things they have done wrong. It is essential that sanctions remain where these are needed, but the thread here is that these are held in balance by a considered opportunity for them to take ownership of a project and to show that they can be reliable and produce good work.

Which brings us back to the Timpson example. The expectation that most of us will produce good work, that sanctions are there when we don't but that if we are trusted we are likely to do the right thing rather than the wrong thing. There is a sense of pride in work done well, and there is also a sense of having been given an opportunity and not wanting to let down those who have given us that opportunity.

And finally...

This series of commentaries on the things which contribute to hopeful settings is intended to open up conversations about what is going well as much as what needs to improve.

'How simple, but how clever...what if we develop some honest and trusted relationships, shine a light on all the best bits and be ready with examples of excellence for all the bits in-between? I wonder what would happen to education and people?'

Dave Sammels, headteacher at Mayflower Academy.

It is through focusing on the good things, the right things that we create the capacity and ability to do more of these. Holding on to hope is worth it for ourselves, our colleagues and most of all for our children.

References

Hart, S., Dixon, A., Drummond, M. J., and McIntyre, D., (2004) *Learning Without Limits*, Open University Press

O'Brien, Jarlath (2016) *Don't Send Him In Tomorrow*, Independent Thinking Press

Peacock, Alison (2016) *Assessment for Learning Without Limits,* Open University Press

Rath, Tom (2009) *Strengths Based Leadership*, Gallup Press

Stobart, Gordon (2014) T*he Expert Learner: Challenging the Myth of Ability,* Open University Press

Weick, Karl E. (1969) *The Social Psychology of Organizing,* McGraw-Hill Higher Education; 2nd edition (1980)